ATHENAZE

An Introduction to Ancient Greek

Revised Edition
Book I

Teacher's Handbook

Maurice Balme
and
Gilbert Lawall

New York   Oxford
OXFORD UNIVERSITY PRESS
1990

Oxford University Press

Oxford   New York   Toronto
Delhi   Bombay   Calcutta   Madras   Karachi
Petaling Jaya   Singapore   Hong Kong   Tokyo
Nairobi   Dar es Salaam   Cape Town
Melbourne   Auckland

and associated companies in
Berlin   Ibadan

Published by Oxford University Press, Inc.,
198 Madison Avenue, New York, New York 10016-4314

Oxford is a registered trademark of Oxford University Press

Library of Congress Cataloging-in-Publication Data
Balme, M. G.
Athenaze / Maurice Balme and Gilbert Lawall.
p.   cm.   English and Ancient Greek.
ISBN 0-19-505621-3 (pbk.).
ISBN 0-19-506384-8   (teacher's handbook)
1. Greek language—Grammar—1950
2. Greek language—Readers.
I. Lawall, Gilbert.   II. Title.
PA258.B325   1990   488.82′421—dc20
89-22967   CIP

11   13   15   17   19   18   16   14   12

Printed in the United States of America
on acid-free paper

CONTENTS

ATHENAZE: SCOPE AND SEQUENCE
Book I: Chapters 1–16

CHAPTER	READINGS			WORD STUDY	ESSAYS	WORD BUILDING	GRAMMAR			
	Daily Life	Mythology	History				Nouns and Pronouns	Adjectives and Participles	Verbs	Misc.
1 Farmer				Derivatives (introductory)	Farmer	Verbs/nouns	Nom., acc., 2nd decl., masc.		3rd sing.	
2 Master, slave				Derivatives (various)	Slavery	Verbs with prepositional prefixes	All cases, sing.: articles, nouns, adjectives; masc.		1st, 2nd, 3rd sing. Imperatives	
3 Plowing and sowing; master, slave, son				Derivatives (lith-, mega-)	Deme and polis	Verbs with prepositional prefixes	All cases, sing., pl.: articles, nouns, adjectives; masc.		3rd pl. Pl. imperatives Infinitives	
4 Wife, daughter, women, at the spring				Derivatives (various)	Women	Nouns/verbs	All cases, sing., pl.: articles, nouns, adjectives; fem. Declensions of nouns Masc. nouns of 1st decl.	Adjectives; regular and irregular	All persons, sing., pl.	Adverbs Definite articles
5	Grandfather, son, dog; chase of hare; slaying of wolf			Derivatives (geo-)	Gods and men	Verbs/nouns	Personal pronouns	Possessive adjectives	-α- contract verbs, active	Elision Attributive and predicate position
6		Theseus, the Minotaur, Ariadne		Derivatives (-phobia)	Myth (Pandora)	Masc./fem. nouns	Uses of dative case		Middle voice and deponents	Prepositions
7		Odysseus and the Cyclops; the death of Aegeus		Derivatives (myth-, the-)	Homer	Nouns/verbs (-άζω, -άζομαι)	3rd decl. consonant stem nouns, adjectives Reflexive pronouns Interrogative and indefinite pronoun and adjective			
8	Journey to city to attend festival	Odysseus and Aeolus		Derivatives (pol-)	Athens (history)	Adverbs of place	3rd decl. nouns with three grades of stem	Participles, present middle	-α- contract verbs, middle	Numbers
9	Arrival in city, visit to Acropolis; procession and sacrifice	Odysseus and Circe		Derivatives (dem-)	Athens (city)	Nouns in -της; adjectives in -τικος	3rd decl., vowel stem: βασιλεύς Uses of genitive case	Participles, present active πᾶς, πᾶσα, πᾶν		

CHAPTER

CHAPTER	READINGS			WORD STUDY	ESSAYS	WORD BUILDING	GRAMMAR			
	Daily Life	Mythology	History				Nouns and Pronouns	Adjectives and Participles	Verbs	Misc.
10	At the theater of Dionysus; the blinding of Philip	Odysseus loses his companions		Derivatives (various)	Festivals	5 sets of verbs and nouns	More 3rd decl. vowel stems: πόλις, ἄστυ		Impersonal verbs	
11	Visit to the doctor		Democedes heals the king	Derivatives (log-)	Greek medicine	Nouns in -της, -σις, and -μα		2nd aorist participles	2nd aorist	
12	To the Piraeus; embarkation for the voyage to Epidaurus		Colaeus discovers Tartessus	Derivatives (math-, ortho-)	Trade and travel	ά-privative		1st aorist participles	1st aorist / Imperfect of εἰμί / Augment of compound verbs	
13	The voyage begins; rough weather; the old sailor to the rescue		Xerxes crosses the Hellespont	Derivatives (naut-, cosm-, astr-)	Rise of Persia	Words from ναυ-	Relative pronouns / 3rd decl. nouns, adjectives with stems in -εσ-: τεῖχος, τριήρης, ἀληθής		Imperfect	Expressions of time
14			The battle of Thermopylae; Artemisium; Greek withdrawal to the Peloponnesus	Derivatives (given names)	Rise of Athens	Military terms		Comparison of adjectives		Comparison of adverbs
15			The battle of Salamis; the Persians capture Athens	Derivatives (mono-)	Aeschylus' *Persians* (Salamis)	Verbs/nouns (ε > ο)	2nd decl. contract nouns: νοῦς		More 2nd aorists: ἔβην, ἔγνων, ἔστην / -o- contract verbs	
16	Athenian naval activity after Salamis; Xerxes' withdrawal to Asia			Derivatives (dyn-)	Athenian Empire	Prefixes ά-, εὐ-, and προ-	More 3rd decl. vowel stems: ναῦς, βοῦς		The verbs δύναμαι, κεῖμαι, ἐπίσταμαι	More numbers

INTRODUCTION

THE COURSE

General Principles

This course was written for use in schools, colleges, and universities with students who have not necessarily been exposed to any other highly inflected language. The course aims at teaching students to read and understand Greek within the context of fifth century Greek civilization and culture. All elements in the course are meant to contribute to this end.

The readings form a continuous story with interwoven subplots. In Chapters 1–20 the narrative consists of made-up Greek; in Chapter 21 and the following chapters the proportion of real Greek increases steadily. The main narrative of each chapter is divided into two parts. Before each narrative is a list of words to be learned, and following each narrative is an explanation of the major new grammar and syntax that have occurred in the reading. Exercises are then provided to give practice with the new linguistic features. In the middle of each chapter is a short essay providing historical and cultural background to the narrative. The reading passages at the end of each chapter form subplots, drawn from Homer's *Odyssey*, Herodotus, and Thucydides.

The narratives are so constructed that students should be able to read and understand the Greek with the help of the vocabulary, the glosses beneath each paragraph, and occasional help from the teacher. Although we believe firmly in the necessity of learning grammar and vocabulary thoroughly, the students' first understanding of the Greek will come from their reading of the story. To this extent their understanding of grammar and syntax will be inductive, and analytical understanding will follow after the presentation of grammar and syntax. This method fosters fluency and confidence and should contribute to the ultimate goal of understanding Greek without translating.

Language Structure

The sentence is the basic unit of sense in any language, and from the start the student should aim at understanding whole sentences within the context of the paragraph as a whole. Sentences in any language follow a limited number of patterns, and students should learn to respond to the elements of the sentence as they appear in sequence, to become sensitive to variations in word order, and to watch inflections closely as keys to structure and meaning.

We have tried to control the input of morphological features and sentence patterns in such a way that the gradient of difficulty remains steady and consistent. The sequence of grammar and syntax is determined by two criteria: (1) what order will the student find easiest? and (2) what order will enable the author to write reasonably interesting Greek as soon as possible?

In any inductive method students are expected to discover some or all of the morphology and syntax as they read and use the language and to develop a personal grammar of their own. In this course that personal awareness is constantly subject to correction and consolidation in the grammatical sections that follow the readings and set forth the grammar in traditional form. Exercises then follow for reinforcement.

The reading passages at any given stage necessarily incorporate grammar that has not been presented formally. At the beginning of the teaching notes for each chapter we list the new grammar that is to be formally presented. These are the features of grammar on which the teacher should concentrate in teaching the reading passages and that will be formally presented in the grammatical sections following the reading passages. Other new features of grammar will be glossed in the notes beneath the paragraphs as necessary, and teachers should not dwell on them or digress into discussion of them. Concentrate on the essential new grammar in the chapter (and on review in any given passage of grammar that has been formally presented earlier).

Vocabulary

Equally, to make rapid progress students must learn vocabulary. We have reinforced important words by constantly reintroducing them in the stories and exercises. Some whole phrases keep recurring, like Homeric formulae. Understanding of some of the basic principles of word building in Greek helps reduce the burden of memory and allows students to attack many new words with confidence.

The vocabulary lists in the chapters give the words that students are expected to learn and be able to use actively both in reading Greek and in translating from English into Greek. Teachers should quiz frequently on this vocabulary, both from Greek to English and from English to Greek.

Many words are glossed at their first occurrence in a reading passage; students are not expected to learn these words thoroughly while reading the paragraph in which they are glossed. Sometimes, however, these words will be used again later in the same passage or in subsequent passages in the same chapter and will usually not be glossed again within that same chapter. If students forget a meaning, they should look back in earlier paragraphs of the same passage or in earlier passages in the same chapter before having recourse to the Greek to English vocabulary at the

end of the book. In the teacher's notes on the reading passages we list words that were glossed earlier in the chapter (see note in this handbook after the final reading in Chapter 1; page 5).

For the principles that govern the vocabulary used in and required by the exercises, see the notes after the answers for Exercise 1a (page 3 of this handbook) and Exercise 1b (page 5). Occasionally translations or vocabulary will be given in parentheses in the sentences of the exercises.

Exercises

The exercises for each chapter include (1) study of English derivatives as an aid to mastery of Greek vocabulary as well as an aid to understanding English (after each α reading), (2) morphological exercises as needed, (3) sentences for translation from and into Greek (sometimes paired, and always utilizing the new morphology, syntax, and vocabulary of the chapter), and (4) exercises on word building within Greek itself (after each β reading).

With regard to English to Greek translation, few would now maintain that "composition" is essential for learning to *read* Greek. It seems, however, to be a most valuable instrument for ensuring a sound knowledge of morphology and syntax.

Tips for Teaching

The two major reading passages (α and β) in each chapter are usually presented, read aloud, translated, and discussed in class as a joint venture undertaken by teacher and students. It is highly recommended that overhead transparencies be made of the reading passages and that the teacher introduce students to the passages by reading them aloud from the projection on the screen. Simple comprehension questions in English will help establish the outlines of the passage, and then it can be approached sentence by sentence with the teacher modeling each sentence and the students repeating after the teacher and translating. The passages are short enough so that they can then be read again by the teacher. In each oral reading (whether by teacher or students) careful attention should be paid to phrasing and tone of voice so that the words are clearly grouped together as appropriate and are spoken in such a way as to convey the meaning of the passage effectively.

We also recommend that teachers encourage their students to study the vocabulary and to reply to the exercise questions *orally*. Not only is the sounding of a language the natural way of learning it, but the combination of the two senses of sight and hearing can greatly facilitate the learning process.

At the end of each chapter are extra passages that are offered not to introduce new vocabulary or grammar, but as exercises in comprehension. These are accompanied by comprehension questions, and it is recommended that the passage be read aloud by the teacher (perhaps again from an overhead projection) and that students be urged to answer the questions (in English or in Greek) without explicitly translating the Greek. One of the purposes of these passages is to get students into the habit of reading Greek for direct comprehension of the ideas expressed; we do not want students to think of Greek only as something that must be translated into English.

The Transition to Unadapted Greek

This course incorporates a gradual but deliberate transition to the reading of unadapted Greek. The old sailor's accounts of Thermopylae and Salamis are based ultimately on Herodotus, using his actual words where possible. Some passages are fairly close to the original, and we include some original lines from Aeschylus' *Persae* and from

Simonides, which are glossed as needed. The reading passages at the ends of Chapters 13–20 follow Herodotus more closely. None of these passages, in our experience, occasions much difficulty, provided the student has a good grasp of participles, on which we lay great emphasis.

The core of Chapters 21–31 consists of adapted extracts from Thucydides, Herodotus, and Plato, with increasing sophistication of syntax and content. In Chapters 21–23 we still use the narrative framework, but as Dicaeopolis and his family are now involved in actual historical events (the outbreak of the Peloponnesian War), we introduce adapted Thucydides. Chapter 23, "The Invasion," follows Thucydides 2.18–23 fairly closely, with cuts. Chapter 24, a digression on the education Philip receives when he is evacuated to Athens, introduces extracts from Plato's *Protagoras*, with very little change. In Chapter 25 we abandon the narrative framework and devote four chapters to Herodotus (the story of Croesus), with each chapter moving closer to the original words. This section ends with Bacchylides' account of the rescue of Croesus by Apollo, which, with glossing, is manageable by students at this stage. Chapters 30 and 31 are based closely on Thucydides II.83–94, with omissions, and the course draws to its close by returning to Dicaeopolis (now the figure in Aristophanes' *Acharnians*) and offering unadapted extracts from Aristophanes' play. By the end of the course all the basic morphology and syntax have been introduced, substantial portions of real Greek have been read, and students are ready to read from annotated texts of the standard authors.

Teaching the Course

This course is intended for use both in secondary schools and in colleges and universities. Its use at both levels will help promote continuity in the study of Greek. It will be completed in different periods of time, depending (among other factors) on the level at which it is being taught, the number of class meetings per week, the length of class periods, and the number of weeks in the semester or quarter. At a relatively rapid pace, the entire course (Books I and II) can be taught in two semesters or three quarters. At a more relaxed pace, the material can be spread out over three semesters or four quarters. If supplemented with extensive background material in history, mythology, and archaeology, the course may be extended to four semesters.

Part of Book I may also be used as a supplement to Latin courses at the advanced levels in the secondary schools. The first ten chapters, for example, might be taught over the course of the entire year of third or fourth year Latin, with one class period per wéek devoted to Greek. Teachers using the course in this way may wish to supplement the material on word study and mythology. Many useful connections can be made with the students' simultaneous study of advanced Latin.

Illustrations

Line drawings, usually based on Greek vases, or photographs are placed before each of the main narratives in Chapters 1–16. The Greek captions illustrate new linguistic features introduced in the chapter. With a little help from the teacher, the meaning of these captions should quickly become apparent to students. The captions are important, since in them students first experience the features of grammar and syntax that enable them to understand the narrative that follows.

Where a painting on a Greek vase fits the caption exactly, our artist reproduced the picture without change. In other cases some adaptation was necessary, and in others scenes have been drawn from imagination in the style of Greek vases.

From Chapter 17 onward, we cease to use line drawings, as we have photographs that fit the captions well enough. We give the sources for all illustrations in the notes in this handbook, with brief descriptions and commentaries as necessary.

Further Reading

We offer the following very brief list of books that will be most useful in teaching Greek from *Athenaze*:

Grammar:

Herbert Weir Smyth. *Greek Grammar*. Revised by Gordon M. Messing. Cambridge: Harvard University Press, 1963.

Word Study:

Kathryn A. Sinkovich. *A Dictionary of English Words from Greek and Latin Roots*. Amherst: *NECN* Publications, 71 Sand Hill Road, Amherst, MA 01002, 1987.

Cultural and Historical Background:

The World of Athens: An Introduction to Classical Athenian Culture. Cambridge, New York: Cambridge University Press, 1984.
John Boardman, Jasper Griffin, and Oswyn Murray, eds. *The Oxford History of the Classical World*. Oxford, New York: Oxford University Press, 1986.

We cite passages in these two books in conjunction with the teacher's notes on the cultural and historical background essays in each chapter of this course.

*　*　*

NOTES TO INTRODUCTION IN STUDENT'S BOOK

Illustration (page vii)

The figure of Myrrhine is based on a painting on a lekythos by the Providence Painter, ca. 470 B.C., in the Ashmolean Museum, Oxford; the figure of Melissa is based on a painting on a dish by the Dish Painter, ca. 460 B.C., in the Hermitage Museum, Leningrad; and the dog is based on a painting on an Attic red figure cup by the Euergides Painter, ca. 500 B.C., in the Ashmolean Museum, Oxford.

Alphabet (page viii)

For further discussion of pronunciation and a demonstration, see the book by W. Sidney Allen and the cassette recording by Stephen Daitz, referred to on pages x–xi. Note that in Greek the difference in pronunciation between short and long vowels is one of quantity rather than quality, thus short ι = peep, and long ι = keen. This is different from the distinction between long and short vowels in Latin, where there is both a qualitative and a quantitative difference. In addition to *but*, the German *Gott* may serve as a model for the pronunciation of omicron.

Students will be interested to know that ὂ μῑκρόν means "small o" and that ὦ μέγα means "big o"; ψῑλόν in ἒ ψῑλόν and ὒ ψῑλόν means "bare," "simple," and differentiated these letters from αι and οι, which represented the sounds in late Greek.

Macrons (page ix top)

Macrons (long marks) have been inserted in the Greek throughout the student's book and the teacher's handbook in order to facilitate accurate pronunciation. Students should be asked to include macrons when they are writing Greek and to consider them, along with accents and breathings, as an integral part of the spelling of Greek words.

It is quite possible that some macrons have been inadvertently omitted. The authors will be grateful to users of these books who inform them of missing macrons.

The markings for long and short vowels are also used in poetic scansion to identify long and short syllables, but poetic scansion is not treated in this book.

Diphthongs (page ix middle)

Students will encounter some words such as νηΐ with a dieresis over the second vowel (see 6α:25); this indicates that the vowels are to be pronounced as two separate syllables and not as a diphthong.

It should be noted that when we speak of diphthongs as being considered long or short (see Reference Grammar, page 208), we are speaking only for purposes of accentuation and not for poetic scansion.

Breathings (pages ix–x):

The rough breathing also occurs over initial ρ, indicating that the ρ should be unvoiced. This is a fine point of pronunciation that may be omitted with beginners.

Practice in Writing and Pronunciation (page xi)

The Greek words and the names of the Muses, Graces, and Fates have been taken from Jane Gray Carter's *Little Studies in Greek* (Silver, Burdett and Company, New York, 1927), pages 63–70 and 101–102. This book is currently available from *NECN* Publications, 71 Sand Hill Road, Amherst, MA 01002.

The following information, taken from Carter's book, may be of use if students ask about the names of the Muses, Graces, and Fates or if you wish to teach their meanings:

Muses:

Κλειώ (κλέω I celebrate), Clio, muse of history

Εὐτέρπη (εὖ + τέρπω I delight), Euterpe, muse of lyric poetry

Θάλεια (θάλλω I bloom), Thalia, muse of comedy

Μελπομένη (μέλπω I sing), Melpomene, muse of tragedy

Τερψιχόρᾱ (τέρπω + χορός), Terpsichore, muse of choral dance and song

Ἐρατώ (ἐρατός lovely from ἐράω I love), Erato, muse of erotic poetry

Πολύμνια (πολύς + ὕμνος), Polyhymnia, muse of the sublime hymn

Οὐρανίᾱ (οὐρανός heaven), Urania, muse of astronomy

Καλλιόπη (καλός + ὄψ voice), Calliope, muse of epic poetry

The Three Graces:

Ἀγλαΐᾱ (ἀγλαός, -ή, -όν shining, splendid), Aglaia, the bright one

Εὐφροσύνη (εὔφρων merry), Euphrosyne, good cheer

Θάλεια (θάλλω I bloom), Thalia, the blooming one

The Three Fates:

Κλωθώ (κλώθω I spin), Spinster, the fate who spins the thread of life

Λάχεσις (λαχεῖν to obtain by lot), Dispenser of Lots

Ἄτροπος (ἀ privative + τρέπω I turn), Inflexible

Illustration (page xiii)

This map shows the mountainous character of Greece and Asia Minor. Cities situated on plains are separated from one another by mountain ranges.

Communication between cities was difficult, and city states with their surrounding villages tended to be fiercely independent. The geography of Greece had a great influence on the character and political life of the people.

* * *

NOTES ON THIS TEACHER'S HANDBOOK

Method of Reference

References to reading passages are made in the following form:

1α:5

This refers to Chapter 1, reading passage α, line 5.

Words Glossed Earlier in Chapters

When words appear again that have been glossed earlier in the chapter, we do not gloss them again, but for the convenience of the teacher we list them in the handbook after the translation of the paragraph in which they appear for the second or third time. We list them in the same format as the original gloss in the student's book, with the Greek word or phrase in boldface and the translation following.

Space for Additional Notes

The material in the following sections of this handbook is carefully coordinated with the sequence of material within each of the chapters of the student's book. Occasionally we have not given notes to particular vocabulary or grammar sections, but in such cases we have left spaces in this handbook for the teacher to jot down notes that may be of use in teaching the material.

ATHENAZE

1
Ο ΔΙΚΑΙΟΠΟΛΙΣ (α)

Title: "Dicaeopolis"

The purposes of this chapter are:

1. Reading: to introduce students to their first passages of Greek reading, which are deliberately simple in order to build confidence, and to introduce the main character of the fictional narrative, the Athenian farmer Dicaeopolis, and to sketch his character, lifestyle, and values
2. Grammar: to present basic forms of verbs (3rd person singular) and of nouns (nominative and accusative cases, second declension masculine) and to introduce the basic uses of the nominative and accusative cases and the concept of agreement
3. Background: to provide some background on the Athenian farmer

Illustration

Photograph of the Moschophoros (Calf-Bearer), ca. 570 B.C. (Athens, Acropolis Museum).

Caption under Illustration

"Dicaeopolis is a farmer; and he is carrying a calf": lead students to deduce the meaning of the caption from the illustration. After reading the caption, ask what the man is doing. This will elicit the meaning of the verb φέρει. Then the question "What is he carrying?" will eventually lead to the answer that it is a calf. Students of art history will be familiar with the statue with the title Moschophorus, and some may remember that this means "Calf-bearer." Then work on the first part of the sentence; students should quickly recognize Δικαιόπολις as a personal name (the capital letter and mention of Dicaeopolis in the Introduction to the book will help). The question "What is he?" will lead to "He's a farmer"

(αὐτουργός is in the vocabulary list), and then the word αὐτουργός may be explained (meaning something like "independent farmer" from αὐτός "himself" and the root ἐργ- seen in τὸ ἔργον "work" and ἐργάζομαι "I work"). The verb ἐστιν will be clear to most students without looking at the vocabulary list.

The caption illustrates grammatical points that are important for this lesson, in particular the use of the nominative case for the subject and the predicate nominative and the use of the accusative case for the direct object.

Vocabulary

In conjunction with teaching the first passage of Greek, point out that οὐκ is used before vowels, how the *postpositive* words are placed in their clauses, and the use of movable ν with ἐστί(ν).

It may be well to point out right away that the definite article is used differently in Greek from in English (see Grammar 2c) and sometimes accompanies proper names (e.g., ὁ Δικαιόπολις) where we would not use it in English.

Translation

Lines 1–9

Dicaeopolis is (an) Athenian; but Dicaeopolis lives not in Athens but in the country; for he is (a) farmer. And so he cultivates the (his) farm and works in the country. But life is hard; for the farm is small, but the work is long. And so Dicaeopolis is always working, and often he groans and says, "O Zeus, life is hard; for the work is endless, and the farm is small and does not provide much food." But the man is strong and energetic; and so he often rejoices; for he is free and (a) farmer, and he loves the (his) home. For the farm is beautiful and provides food, not much but enough. [As comprehension and then translation of the passage are worked out in class, students will need to be informed of three important points: (1) that the indefinite article often needs to be supplied in English translation, (2) that the definite article often serves the function of a possessive adjective in English ("his farm," "his life," and "his home"), (3) that the Greek definite article is often not translated into English ("O Zeus, life is hard"), and (4) that a pronominal subject often has to be supplied in English translation, e.g., αὐτουργὸς γάρ ἐστιν = "for *he* is a farmer." All of these points will need to be kept in mind when students do the exercises in translation from Greek to English and English to Greek.

In lines 7–8, note that Dicaeopolis "often rejoices" both because he is free and because he is an αὐτουργός—more than simply "a farmer," a farmer who works *his own land*, as opposed to a hired laborer or a slave.]

Word Study

The purposes of the Word Study and Word Building exercises are (1) to improve the student's understanding of English, (2) to show links between ancient Greek and modern Western culture, and (3) to improve the student's Greek vocabulary. In the first few chapters we give rather full explanations of the formation of the English words, illustrating principles that apply to words appearing in later exercises. The following points on the formation of English words from Greek may be helpful:

1. Some words are unchanged from their Greek forms, e.g., *metropolis* = ἡ μητρόπολις; *drama* = τὸ δρᾶμα.
2. Sometimes words are unchanged except for the omission of the Greek noun ending, e.g., *graph* = ἡ γραφή; *emblem* = τὸ ἔμβλημα; and *despot* = ὁ δεσπότης.
3. The Greek ending -ίᾱ is regularly replaced by *-y* in English, e.g., ἡ φιλοσοφίᾱ becomes *philosophy*.
4. The suffixes *-er* and *-ian* are regularly added to a Greek stem to de-

note the agent, e.g., *philosoph-er* (ὁ φιλόσοφ-ος; *politic-ian* (πολῑτικ-ός).
5. The suffix *-al* is added to a Greek stem to form an adjective, e.g., *politic-al* (πολῑτικ-ός).
6. The suffix *-ist*, e.g., *anthropolog-ist*, properly speaking corresponds to the Greek agent suffix added to the stems of verbs ending in -ιζ-, e.g., λογ-ίζ-ομαι = I calculate, ὁ λογιστής = *calculator, auditor*; it is extended in English, being added to nouns and adjectives to designate the person concerned with or devoted to some school, principle, or art, e.g., *athe-ist* (derived from the adjective ἄθεος, -ον).

It should be noted that although many English words are derived from ancient Greek words, there are also many coinages, correctly formed especially from the seventeenth century onwards, e.g., *megaphone* (μέγα + ἡ φωνή); *lithograph* (ὁ λίθος + ἡ γραφή). There are also some incorrectly formed, i.e., hybrid words, such as *television* (τῆλε "far" + *vision* from Latin *videō*). New coinages are continually being made, especially in the sciences and medicine, to express new concepts, e.g., *autistic*, too new to appear in *The Oxford English Dictionary*. The flexibility of the Greek language makes it possible to express a complex idea in a single word.

The figures in parentheses after the English words give the date when the word first appeared in English writings.

1. *anthropology* (1593, a coinage): ὁ ἄνθρωπος + ὁ λόγος, -λογίᾱ = "the study of mankind." (The Greek author Philo, 2nd century B.C., has ἀνθρωπολογέω.)
2. *polysyllabic* (1782, a coinage; the noun *polysyllable* appeared in 1589): πολύς + ἡ συλλαβή "that which is taken together," used by ancient grammarians, "syllable." (The word πολυσύλλαβος, -ον occurs in Lucian, 2nd century A.D.)

3. *philosophy*: φιλο- + ἡ σοφίᾱ, ἡ
   φιλοσοφίᾱ "love of wisdom,"
   "philosophy."
4. *microscope* (1656, a coinage):
   μῑκρός, -ά, -όν + σκοπέω, ἡ σκοπή =
   "an instrument for observing small
   things." The word was coined when
   the instrument was invented.

Grammar 1

It should be emphasized that verb
forms such as λύει can be translated as
simple presents (loosens), as progres-
sive (is loosening), or as emphatic (does
loosen). The latter will be needed when
the simple present is used in a question
(does he loosen . . . ?).

Grammar 2

It may be useful to explain the difference between natural gender and
grammatical gender at this point. If
students wonder why we say "Nouns are
usually *masculine* or *feminine* or *neuter*,
mention a word such as κύων "dog,"
which can be either masculine or feminine, depending on the sex of the dog.

Students may need some practice in
identifying the parts of speech: verbs,
nouns, adjectives, prepositions, adverbs,
conjunctions, and so forth. If necessary,
have students locate the words in the
story under their rubrics in the vocabulary list on page 2.

It may be useful in analyzing the
structure of sentences to introduce symbols such as S (subject), LV (linking
verb), and C (complement) to clarify the
structure of sentences such as the first
example in Grammar 2b, and S
(subject), V (verb), and O (object) to rep-
resent sentences of the second type.
Later the symbols can become more
complex: e.g., TV for transitive verb, IT
for intransitive verb, and DO and IO for
direct and indirect objects. Have students associate S and C with the nominative case, O or DO with the accusative,
and IO with the dative.

After studying the distinction in
form and function between nominative
and accusative cases, students may be
invited to go back to the story and locate
the second declension nouns in nominative and accusative cases and to observe the use of nominative for subject
and accusative for direct object.

Exercise 1a

1. The work is long.
   ὁ οἶκός ἐστι μῑκρός.
2. The house is beautiful.
   ἰσχῡρός ἐστιν ὁ ἄνθρωπος.
3. Dicaeopolis loves his home.
   ὁ ἄνθρωπος τὸν σῖτον παρέχει.
4. The farm provides much food.
   πολὺν πόνον παρέχει ὁ κλῆρος.
5. The man does not work in the country.
   ὁ Δικαιόπολις οὐκ οἰκεῖ ἐν ταῖς
   Ἀθήναις.

Note that in all exercises we use
primarily the vocabulary that is given
in the vocabulary lists preceding the
reading passages (this is the vocabulary
that students are expected to learn actively). Sometimes we use words that
have been glossed in the reading passages in the chapter in which the exercises occur; these words may also be
found in the vocabularies at the end of
the book. Occasionally exercises will
contain words that students are expected
to deduce. These will be pointed out in
the teacher's notes and are also always
included in the vocabularies at the end of
the book. In short, students should be
familiar with or should be able to deduce
all vocabulary in the exercises, but in
case they encounter problems they can
find the vocabulary at the end of the
book.

Vocabulary for all English to Greek
exercises is given in the English to
Greek vocabulary list at the end of the
book. Students should, however, be
urged to find the words in the chapter vocabulary lists and in the glosses and to

use the end vocabulary only as a last resort.

Note that students will need to know some of the principles affecting accents and their use with enclitics before doing the English to Greek sentences (enclitics in sentences 1 and 2). Students should examine these principles briefly in the Reference Grammar at the end of the student's book (pages 208–209; see in particular a and e under Enclitics on page 209) before doing this exercise. The rules for accents should be learned gradually, partly from observation of their use in the stories and exercises and partly from study of the rules. Do not overwhelm students with all the rules at the beginning.

In exercises where there are pairs of sentences for translation from and into Greek, we have in the translations of the English sentences given the same word order as that of the parallel Greek sentence; it is useful to encourage students to vary the word order, and you may accept any grammatically correct version, e.g.:

2. ὁ ἄνθρωπός ἐστιν ἰσχῡρός.
4. ὁ κλῆρος πολὺν πόνον παρέχει.
    ὁ κλῆρος παρέχει πολὺν πόνον.

The Athenian Farmer

Illustration (page 6)

The illustration shows a detail from an Attic black figure cup by Nicosthenes, ca. 520 B.C. (Berlin, Antikenmuseum, Staatliche Museen).

Illustration (page 7)

The photograph was taken by D. A. Harissiades, Athens.

For further reading, see *The World of Athens*, pp. 62–71 and 178–179. Further background reading: Aristophanes' *Acharnians* and Menander's *Dyskolos*.

Ο ΔΙΚΑΙΟΠΟΛΙΣ (β)

Illustration

Drawn from imagination, based on an Attic black figure cup of the Burgon Group, sixth century B.C. (London, British Museum). See also the illustrations for 2α, 2β, 3α, and 3β.

Caption under Illustration

"Dicaeopolis lifts a large stone and carries it out of the field": encourage students to deduce the new phrases μέγαν λίθον and ἐκ τοῦ ἀγροῦ from the illustration. Students will find the new verbs αἴρει and φέρει in the vocabulary list (they have already met φέρει in the caption under the illustration for passage α). You may prefer to read the story first and come back to the caption afterwards; highlight the subject, the direct object, and the prepositional phrase.

Vocabulary

Verbs of motion are given special attention in this course, and effort will be made in the teacher's notes to sort out the meanings and usages of the various verbs. The verb βαδίζω means "to walk," as opposed to running or sailing, but it has a more general meaning of "to go" or "to proceed (toward or against)." We use it primarily in contexts where walking is clearly implied.

Translation

Lines 1–8

Dicaeopolis is working in the field; for he is digging the field. The toil is long and hard; for he is carrying (the) stones out of the field. He lifts a big stone and carries (it) to the stone heap. The man is strong, but he works for a long time and is very tired. For the sun is blazing and wears him out. And so he sits under the tree and rests for not a long (= a short) time. For he soon gets up and works. Finally the sun sets. And

so Dicaeopolis no longer works but walks toward (his) home.
[In the sentence τοὺς γὰρ λίθους ἐκ τοῦ ἀγροῦ φέρει (2) the definite article (τούς) is used where we would not use it in English.

In the sentence μέγαν λίθον αἴρει καὶ φέρει πρὸς τὸ ἕρμα (3) a pronominal object of the verb φέρει must be supplied in English; students should be alerted to the fact that the object in such cases may be omitted in Greek.]

Word Building

1. He/she lives, dwells; house, home, dwelling
2. He/she works; toil, work
3. He/she farms; farmer
4. He/she loves; dear one, friend

These pairs of verb and noun are formed from a common root, e.g., πον-, to which -ε- is added in the verbal form (πον-έ-ω) and -ο- in the noun form (πόν-ο-ς).

Ο ΚΛΗΡΟΣ

Title: "The Farm"

The word was glossed in passage α:2–3.

Translation

Lines 1–3
The work is long and hard. But the farmer does not shirk but always cultivates his farm. For the farm is beautiful and provides much food. And so the man rejoices; for he is strong and is not often tired.
[Note that words or phrases that have been glossed once in a chapter are not glossed again in the same chapter. They will, however, be found in the Greek to English vocabulary at the end of the book, and they will be listed in the teacher's notes for convenience. Students should be encouraged to look back at the earlier readings if they need help with these words or phrases and to use

the vocabulary at the end of the book only as a last resort.

Words and phrases glossed earlier in chapter: αἰεί always   γεωργεῖ farms   τὸν κλῆρον the (= his) farm   παρέχει provides   πολλάκις often   κάμνει is tired.

Call attention to the elision between the words ἀλλ' αἰεί (= ἀλλὰ αἰεί). Students should be encouraged to use elision in Exercise 1b, no. 4 below, and they should be alert to elisions in the subsequent reading passages. Elision is treated formally in Chapter 5, Grammar 4, page 45.

The comprehension questions that follow the final reading passages in each chapter may be used in several ways. They may be answered in English, or students may answer them with Greek words or phrases from the story. In any case, the final passages are offered above all as exercises in reading and comprehension, rather than in mechanical translation. Sometimes the questions will aid comprehension by providing clues to the context and the overall structure of a sentence in the reading. After the passages have been used for practice in reading and comprehension in class, they may be assigned as written translation exercises for homework, along with the final English to Greek sentences.]

Exercise 1b

1. ὁ Δικαιόπολις αὐτουργός ἐστιν.
   ὁ Δικαιόπολίς ἐστιν αὐτουργός.
2. αἰεὶ πονεῖ ἐν τῷ ἀγρῷ.
3. πολλάκις οὖν κάμνει· μακρὸς γάρ ἐστιν ὁ πόνος.
4. ἀλλ' οὐκ ὀκνεῖ· φιλεῖ γὰρ τὸν οἶκον.

Most of the vocabulary for these final English to Greek exercises comes from the vocabulary lists that precede the reading passages (containing words students are expected to master). Some of it comes from words glossed in the three sets of readings in the chapter. All needed vocabulary for these English to

Greek translations is given in the English to Greek vocabulary at the end of the book, but students should be urged to locate words in the chapter vocabularies and readings and not to rely on the English to Greek vocabulary at the end of the book.

2
Ο ΞΑΝΘΙΑΣ (α)

Title: "Xanthias"

The purposes of this chapter are:

1. Reading: to introduce Dicaeopolis's slave, Xanthias, his personality, and his interaction with his master
2. Grammar: (α) to present 1st, 2nd, and 3rd person singular verb forms and the singular imperative and (β) to present second declension nouns (masculine and neuter) in all cases in the singular with accompanying articles and adjectives and to describe the basic uses of the cases
3. Word Building: to present examples of verbs compounded with prepositional prefixes and to teach students to deduce their meaning wherever possible
4. Background: to present a discussion of the institution of slavery in the Greek world

Illustration

See note on illustration for 1β (see above, page 4).

Caption under Illustration

"Dicaeopolis drives the ox, and the slave carries the plow": to elicit the meaning of the first half of the sentence, simply ask, "What is Dicaeopolis doing?" while pointing at him and the ox in the picture. It may take students unacquainted with country life a few moments to come up with the word *ox*; if they cannot deduce the meaning of ἐλαύνει from the picture, they will quickly find it in the vocabulary list. The question "What is Xanthias doing?" will elicit the answer that he is carrying something, but the identity of the object may require further questioning or a glance at the vocabulary list. The question "Who is Xanthias?" will quickly bring the answer "He's a slave," especially from students with an eye on the vocabulary list.

The caption introduces the neuter noun (in the first chapter all nouns were masculine, with the exception of the word for Athens). It is also a good example of the μέν . . . δέ. . . . correlation introduced in this chapter, and it reinforces the third person singular verb endings introduced in the first chapter.

Vocabulary

Note that we use ἐκβαίνει in the limited sense "he/she steps out, comes out"; it is generally followed in the stories with a prepositional phrase, e.g., ἐκ τοῦ οἴκου "out of the house." Later the verb will be used with ἐκ τῆς νεώς in the sense "to disembark."

We introduce the aorist imperative ἐλθέ as a vocabulary item (it needs no explanation at this stage).

Translation

Lines 1–10

Dicaeopolis steps/comes out of the house and calls Xanthias. Xanthias is a slave, a strong but lazy man (a man strong on the one hand, but lazy on the other hand); for he does not work unless Dicaeopolis is present. And now he is sleeping in the house. And so Dicaeopolis calls him and says, "Come here, (O) Xanthias. Why are you sleeping? Don't be so lazy but hurry!" And so Xanthias steps/comes slowly out of the house and says, "Why are you so hard, master? For I am not lazy but am already hurrying." But Dicaeopolis says, "Come here and help. (For) take the plow and carry it to the field. For I am driving the oxen. But hurry! For the field is small, but the work is long."

[In the translation of the second sentence (1–3) we include the words "on the one hand . . . on the other hand" in the version given in parentheses, but normally the translations will not include renderings of μέν ... δέ. ... These particles are regularly used in Greek whenever there are parallel or antithetical sentences, clauses, or phrases; μέν warns the listener or reader that there will be a second parallel or contrasted item to be introduced later. Students should be encouraged to appreciate how these words correlate the sentences, clauses, or phrases in which they occur, but the words need not be translated each time.

Students should be reminded that verbs such as καθεύδει (3) can be translated "sleeps," "is sleeping," or "does sleep," depending on the context and that Greek does not make the distinctions in meaning that English is able to make by using these different forms of the verb.

With the direct address in lines 4–5 ("ἐλθὲ δεῦρο, ὦ Ξανθίᾱ. διὰ τί καθεύδεις;"), we begin to introduce important new verbal concepts: the singular imperative (ἐλθέ, 4), second person singular verb forms (καθεύδεις, 5; εἶ, 6), and finally first person singular verb forms (εἰμι, σπεύδω, 7). The context of the dialogue should make the new forms clear without need for formal discussion; let students discover the new forms and deduce their meaning for themselves, and let discussion wait until the grammar section.

The ὦ that accompanies the vocative in line 4 will allow students to deduce the meaning of the words here without being told about the vocative case. They have already seen the nominative case of the slave's name, which they should use in their translation. The word ὦ is translated once above (in parentheses) but will not be translated henceforth and need not be translated by students.

Attention should be given to how the word γάρ implies a causal connection between the statement in which it occurs and what has come before. Usually the connection is obvious, but in Dicaeopolis' commands ἐλθὲ δεῦρο καὶ βοήθει· λάμβανε γὰρ τὸ ἄροτρον. ... (8) the

connection is not so obvious. We might make the connection explicit by translating "Come here and help. For I want you to take the plow. ... " Simpler English would say, "Come here and help. Take the plow. ... " Students should be urged to pay attention to the connections between clauses and sentences in the Greek readings.]

Word Study

1. *despotic*: ὁ δεσπότης, δεσποτικός, -ή, -όν. ὁ δεσπότης = "a master" (of slaves), then "a despot," "absolute ruler" (*despot* 1562, *despotic* 1608). *chronology* (coined, 1593): ὁ χρόνος + ὁ λόγος, -λογίᾱ).

2. *dendrologist* (coined, 1708): τὸ δένδρον + ὁ λόγος, -λογίᾱ + -ιστης (λογίζομαι, ὁ λογιστής).

3. *heliocentric* (coined, 1667): ὁ ἥλιος + τὸ κέντρον "any sharp point, horse-goad, ox-goad, point of a spear, sting of a bee, stationary point of a pair of compasses, center of a circle," cf. Latin *centrum*. The heliocentric theory of the universe, that the sun is at the center, is opposed to the geo-centric theory that the earth (ἡ γῆ) is at the center.

4. *chronometer* (coined, 1735): ὁ χρόνος + τὸ μέτρον "measurement"; an instrument for measuring time.

Grammar 1

Have students practice with the other verbs they have had: ἐκβαίνει, ἐλαύνει, καθεύδει, λαμβάνει, λέγει, σπεύδει, φέρει, and χαίρει; and the contract verbs καλεῖ, οἰκεῖ, πονεῖ, and φιλεῖ.

Exercise 2a

1. I am calling/I call the slave.
2. The slave is working in the house.
3. Why aren't you hurrying?
4. I am not lazy.
5. You are strong.
6. He/she is carrying the plow.
7. I am hurrying to the field.

8. Why are you calling the slave?
9. The slave is lazy.
10. The slave is stepping out/coming
    out of the house.

Exercise 2b

1. οὐ σπεύδει.
2. διὰ τί οὐ πονεῖς;
3. τὸ ἄροτρον φέρω.
4. πρὸς τὸν ἀγρὸν σπεύδεις.
5. ῥᾴθῡμός ἐστιν.
6. οὐκ ἰσχῡρός εἰμι.
7. οὐκ εἶ δοῦλος.
8. ὁ δοῦλος οὐ πονεῖ.
9. ὁ δοῦλος φέρει τὸ ἄροτρον πρὸς τὸν
    ἀγρόν.
10. ῥᾴθῡμός εἰμι.

These English to Greek sentences
may be difficult for some students at this
stage; it may be useful to preview the exercise before assigning it or to do half of
the sentences together in class and as-
sign the other half for written work.
    Students may need to be reminded
that the subject pronouns in the English
sentences need not be translated with
separate words in Greek but are ac-
counted for by the endings of the verbs.

Grammar 2

After students have studied both of
the grammar sections and done the accompanying exercises, go back through
the reading passage at the beginning of
the chapter and have students identify
each verb form (indicative/imperative,
and 1st, 2nd, or 3rd person for the indicative forms). If overhead transparencies are used, highlight the verb
forms with colored markers.

Exercise 2c

1. Come out of the house, Xanthias, and
    come here!
2. Don't sleep, slave, but work!
3. Don't be so hard, master!
4. Take the plow and hurry to the field!
5. Call the slave, master!

Four vocatives are included in the
sentences above, but at this stage it is
sufficient for students to recognize the
vocative from the preceding ὦ. The
vocative of second declension nouns will
be presented in the second half of this
chapter, and the vocative of third
declension masculine nouns, in Chapter 4, Grammar 3, page 38. Do not get
into discussion of the forms now.

Slavery

Illustration (page 13)

Detail of an Attic red figure stamnos
by the Pig Painter, ca. 460 B.C.
(Fitzwilliam Museum, Cambridge,
England).

Illustration (page 15 top)

Clay plaque from a shrine near the
potters' quarter at Corinth, sixth century
B.C. (Berlin, Staatliche Museen). A jug
of water is lowered to the workmen in the
pit.

Illustration (page 15 bottom)

Detail of an Attic red figure column
crater, called the "Orchard Vase," ca.
460 B.C. (New York, Metropolitan Museum).

For further reading, see *The World
of Athens*, pp. 153–157 for population figures, pp. 158–188 for slavery, and pp.
188–190 for metics. See also *The Oxford
History of the Classical World*, Chapter 9,
"Life and Society in Classical Greece."

Ο ΞΑΝΘΙΑΣ (β)

Illustration

See note on illustration for 1β (see
above, page 4).

Caption under Illustration

Dicaeopolis says, "Hurry, Xanthias,
and bring me the plow": all of the words
are familiar except μοι, which is glossed

under the first paragraph of the reading; encourage students to deduce it in the caption.

Vocabulary

Note that beginning with this vocabulary list verbs are given in the first person singular.

Note that for the preposition εἰς we give three meanings, "into," "to," and "at." Students should be warned from the outset that Greek words may be equivalent to more than one English word. In particular, the use of prepositions in both Greek and English is complex. Students should become familiar with the area of meaning of a preposition and then be urged to observe closely how prepositions are used in context with particular verbs to express certain definite ideas.

Translation

Lines 1–10

And so Dicaeopolis drives the oxen, and Xanthias walks behind and carries the plow. And soon Dicaeopolis leads the oxen into the field and looks toward the slave; but Xanthias is not present; for he is going slowly. And so Dicaeopolis calls him and says, "Hurry up, Xanthias, and bring (to) me the plow." But Xanthias says, "But I'm already hurrying, master; why are you so hard?" And he slowly carries the plow toward him. And so Dicaeopolis leads the oxen under the yoke and attaches the plow. (And) then he looks toward the slave; but Xanthias isn't there; for he is sleeping under the tree.

[The plural definite article and noun are used in τοὺς βοῦς (3, 8), but let students deduce the meaning here and leave discussion until the next chapter. Concentrate on the singulars, second declension, masculine and neuter: τὸ ἄροτρον (2), τὸν ἀγρόν (3), τὸν δοῦλον (3), τὸ ἄροτρον (5, 7), τὸ ζυγόν (8), τὸν δοῦλον (9), and τῷ δένδρῳ (9–10).

English is more sparing in its use of connecting particles than Greek; ἔπειτα δέ (8) will be adequately rendered by "then" rather than "and then" in the last sentence.]

Lines 11–17

And so Dicaeopolis calls him and says, "Come here, cursed creature. Don't sleep but help; (for) take the seed and walk behind." And so the slave takes the seed and walks behind, and the master calls Demeter and says, "Be gracious, Demeter, and multiply the seed." Then he takes the goad and goads the oxen and says, "Hurry, oxen; drag the plow and plow the field."

[ἵλαος (14): there is no need to discuss two-termination adjectives at this stage.

At the end of this paragraph (16–17) three plural imperatives are used: σπεύδετε, ἕλκετε, and ἀροτρεύετε. Students may not notice the new forms because the context makes the meaning clear; the plural imperatives will be formally introduced in the next chapter (Chapter 3, Grammar 1b, p. 22). Students are to deduce the meaning of the verb ἀροτρεύετε from their knowledge of the noun ἄροτρον.]

Word Building

1. He/she carries to(ward).
2. He/she carries out.
3. He/she drives toward.
4. He/she steps toward, approaches.
5. He/she calls out.

Grammar 3

Students have met the following prepositional phrases with the genitive case in the readings: ἐκ τοῦ ἀγροῦ (1β:2), δι' ὀλίγου (1β:6, 2β:2), and ἐκ τοῦ οἴκου (2α:1, 6).

Exercise 2d

1. τὸν 2. τῷ 3. ὁ 4. τοῦ 5. τὸ 6. τῷ 7. τῷ

Exercise 2e

1. ὁ δοῦλος σπεύδει πρὸς τὸν ἀγρόν.
   The slave hurries to the field.
2. ὁ Δικαιόπολις τὸν ῥᾴθυμον δοῦλον
   καλεῖ.
   Dicaeopolis calls the lazy slave.
3. ἐλθὲ δεῦρο καὶ βοήθει.
   Come here and help!
4. ἐγὼ ἐλαύνω τοὺς βοῦς ἐκ τοῦ ἀγροῦ.
   I am driving the oxen out of the field.
5. μὴ χαλεπὸς ἴσθι, ὦ δοῦλε, ἀλλὰ
   πόνει.
   Don't be difficult, slave, but work!

Exercise 2f

1. The slave is not Athenian.
   ὁ Ξανθίας οὐκ ἔστιν ἰσχῦρός.
2. Dicaeopolis steps/comes out of the
   house and calls the slave.
   ὁ δοῦλος σπεύδει πρὸς τὸν ἀγρὸν
   καὶ φέρει τὸ ἄροτρον.
3. The slave is not helping but sleeping under the tree.
   ὁ ἄνθρωπος οὐ πονεῖ ἀλλὰ βαδίζει
   πρὸς τὸν οἶκον.
4. Go into the house, Xanthias, and
   bring the food.
   σπεῦδε, ὦ δοῦλε, καὶ ἐξέλαυνε τοὺς
   βοῦς.
5. Don't sleep, Xanthias, but help.
   μὴ δεῦρο ἐλθέ, ὦ ἄνθρωπε, ἀλλὰ
   πόνει ἐν τῷ ἀγρῷ.

Note the accent on the phrase οὐκ
ἔστιν in no. 1.
   In no. 4, students are to deduce
εἴσελθε from what they learned in Word
Building on page 17.
   In no. 4 we supply the verb ἐξελαύνω
in the student's book, in the first person
singular. Students must be warned that

they need to convert glosses such as this
into the correct form for the context.

Ο ΔΟΥΛΟΣ

Title: "The Slave"

Translation

Lines 1–6

The farmer hurries into the field
and calls the slave. But the slave is not
there; for he is sleeping under the tree.
And so the master walks toward him
and says, "Come here, you lazy slave,
and help!" And so the slave walks toward him and says, "Don't be hard
master; for I am now here and I am carrying the plow to you." And so the master says, "Hurry, Xanthias; for the field
is small but the work is long."
[Words glossed earlier in chapter: ὑπό
under   δεῦρο here   ῥᾴθυμε lazy.]

Exercise 2g

1. ὁ Δικαιόπολις οὐκέτι πονεῖ ἀλλὰ
   λύει τοὺς βοῦς.
2. ἔπειτα δὲ τὸν δοῦλον καλεῖ καὶ
   λέγει· "μηκέτι πόνει ἀλλὰ δεῦρο ἐλθὲ
   καὶ λάμβανε τὸ ἄροτρον. ἐγὼ μὲν
   γὰρ τοὺς βοῦς πρὸς τὸν οἶκον
   ἐλαύνω, σὺ δὲ φέρε τὸ ἄροτρον."
3. ὁ μὲν οὖν Δικαιόπολις ἐλαύνει τοὺς
   βοῦς ἐκ τοῦ ἀγροῦ, ὁ δὲ δοῦλος τὸ
   ἄροτρον λαμβάνει καὶ φέρει πρὸς
   τὸν οἶκον.

In no. 1, students are to produce λύει,
which is not given in the vocabularies
but in the paradigms of forms.
   In no. 3, note the use of μέν with Dicaeopolis, looking forward to δέ with the
slave.

3
Ο ΑΡΟΤΟΣ (α)

Title: "The Plowing"

Try to get students to deduce the meaning of the title from their knowledge of τὸ ἄροτρον and the illustration.

The purposes of this chapter are:

1. Reading: (α) to continue the description of the interaction of master and slave in a typical situation on the farm and (β) to introduce Dicaeopolis's son, Philip, and to show these two members of the family and the slave working together on a common project
2. Grammar (α) to continue filling in the verb forms by introducing the 3rd person plural, the plural imperatives, and the infinitives and (β) to introduce all plural forms of second declension masculine and neuter nouns with articles and adjectives
3. Word Building: to continue the study of compound verbs from the previous chapter
4. Background: to present a discussion of the life of farmers in the towns or demes of Attica and of their relationship to the mother city, Athens

Illustration

Drawn from an Attic black figure cup of the Burgon Group, sixth century B.C. (London, British Museum). Illustrations for 1β, 2α, 2β, and 3β are based on this cup.

Caption under Illustration

"Dicaeopolis drives the oxen, and the oxen drag the plow": the first part of the sentence will be familiar, but the second part introduces plural forms that the students will meet in this chapter for the first time. Make sure they realize that there are two oxen in this picture, and then ask what the oxen are doing

("they are dragging the plow"; this verb was glossed in passage 2β:16). Calling attention to the plural forms here will make it easy for students to recognize the plural forms introduced in the first paragraph of the reading.

Vocabulary

The verb μένω may be translated several ways; in the story that follows it is used of the oxen that are stopped and standing still because of a stone that impedes the plow. "Are waiting" may be used to translate the verb, but other translations such as "are idle," "are stopped," or "are standing still" could be used. The idea is that the oxen have come to a stop and are temporarily motionless, inactive, or idle.

Note that we use προσχωρέω with the dative case (the first occurrence with the dative case is in Exercise 3c no. 3).

The postpositive placement of the verb φησί(ν) is explained in the first note under the first paragraph of the translation just below. It is best explained to students in conjunction with an example in the reading passage.

Translation

Lines 1–9

Dicaeopolis is driving the oxen, and the oxen are dragging the plow, and Xanthias is sowing the seed. But look! The oxen are waiting/are idle and no longer drag the plow. And so Dicaeopolis calls the oxen and, "Hurry up, oxen," he says; "Don't wait!" But the oxen are still waiting. And so Dicaeopolis says, "Why are you waiting, oxen?" and looks at the plow, and look! a stone is obstructing it. And so Dicaeopolis takes (hold of) the stone but does not lift it; for it is big. And so he calls the slave, and, "Come here, Xanthias," he says, "and help! For a big stone is obstructing the plow, and the oxen are waiting/are idle."

[The word φησί(ν) is postpositive (like *inquit* in Latin), that is, it is placed in the middle of or after a direct quotation, not before it. Sometimes we preserve this order in the translations, but usually it is not possible to do so.

Note that ἐμποδίζει (9) consists of ἐν and the root of the word for "foot," ποδ- and originally referred to putting the feet in bonds or fetters.]

Lines 10–15

And so Xanthias slowly approaches, but he does not help; for he looks at the stone and, "The stone is big, master," he says; "Look! it is not possible to lift it." But Dicaeopolis says, "Don't be lazy but help. For it is possible to lift the stone." And so together (both) the master and the slave lift the stone and are carrying it out of the field.

[Be sure students appreciate the effect of the word order in "μέγας ἐστὶν ὁ λίθος" (11), with the adjective placed first because it is most important in Xanthias' thinking.

This paragraph introduces the infinitive (αἴρειν, 12, 13), used twice after δυνατόν ἐστιν. Allow students to grasp the meaning of the infinitive from the context. There is another example in the next paragraph: οὐ δυνατόν ἐστιν αὐτὸν φέρειν (21).

Greek almost invariably uses τε with the first member of a pair of things or persons, thus ὅ τε δεσπότης καὶ ὁ δοῦλος (14); English is far more sparing in its use of "both . . . and," only inserting "both" for emphasis. Thus, we have put the "both" in parentheses, and students need not always include it in their translations.]

Lines 16–25

While they are carrying it, Xanthias stumbles and drops the stone; and the stone falls upon Dicaeopolis's foot. And so Dicaeopolis groans and says, "Zeus, oh my poor foot! Take (hold of) the stone, you fool, and lift it and don't be so clumsy." But Xanthias says, "Why are you so hard, master? *I* am not to blame. For the stone is big, and it is not possible to carry it." But Dicaeopolis

says, "Don't talk nonsense, you jailbird, but lift the stone and carry (it) out of the field." And so they again lift the stone and with difficulty carry it out of the field. Then Dicaeopolis drives the oxen, and the oxen wait no longer/are no longer idle but drag the plow.

[The long phrase πρὸς τὸν τοῦ Δικαιοπόλεως πόδα (17) should be pronounced with care as a unit to be sure that students take all of the words together as a single phrase. A comprehension question may help: "On whose foot did the stone land?" After the phrase has been comprehended as a unit it should be analyzed into its parts, showing how the genitive is sandwiched in between the article and noun.

φεῦ τοῦ ποδός (18): "oh my poor foot!" Exclamations regularly go into the genitive case (genitive of cause).

ὦ ἀνόητε (19): "you fool"; the word "you" is often a good rendering of ὦ.

οὐ γὰρ αἴτιός εἰμι ἐγώ (20–21): "*I* am not to blame"; note the insertion of ἐγώ for emphasis.

ὦ μαστῑγίᾱ (22): "you jailbird"; this is a regular term of abuse in the comedies of Aristophanes; it means literally one who deserves a *whipping*.

ἔκφερε ἐκ τοῦ ἀγροῦ (23): "carry (it) out of the field." Here and in the next sentence note the redundancy of the prepositional prefix on the verb and the prepositional phrase. Remember that compound verbs such as this where the meaning of the compound is obvious are not given in the vocabulary lists; students should become accustomed to deducing the meaning of these compound verbs (see Chapter 2, Word Building, page 17). Students may wish to keep a list of their own of such verbs, because it will come in handy in some of the English to Greek translation exercises, e.g., Exercise 3g, no. 2, p. 29.]

Word Study

1. *lithograph* (coined, 1825): ὁ λίθος + γράφω "I write, draw," ἡ γραφή

"drawing." A lithograph is an art work produced from a drawing on stone.

2. *monolith* (coined, 1848): μόνος, -η, -ον "alone, only" + ὁ λίθος. Monolith is the archaeological term for a single stone as opposed to a circle of stones. Your students may have met this word in the adjectival form *monolithic* in political contexts, e.g., "the monolithic state." You might ask them what this means and how the word has acquired this particular meaning.

3. *megalithic* (coined, 1839): μέγας + ὁ λίθος. "Built of large stones," like Stonehenge.

4. *megaphone* (coined by the inventor, Edison, 1838): μέγας + ἡ φωνή "voice."

Grammar 1

This is a good time to begin pointing out that the accent of verbs is recessive.

Exercise 3a

αἴρειν (12, 13), φέρειν (21).

Exercise 3b

1. The oxen are no longer dragging the plow.
2. Dicaeopolis and the slave approach and look at the plow.
3. Dicaeopolis says, "Look! a big stone is obstructing the plow."
4. Lift the stone and carry (it) out of the field.
5. But the slave says, "Look! it is a big stone; it is not possible to lift it."
6. (Both) Dicaeopolis and the slave lift the stone and carry (it) out of the field.
7. Don't wait/Don't be idle, oxen, but hurry up!
8. The oxen are no longer waiting/idle but again drag the plow.

Exercise 3c

1. οἱ βόες ἐν τῷ ἀγρῷ καθεύδουσιν.

2. ἔλθετε δεῦρο καὶ ἐξελαύνετε τοὺς βοῦς, ὦ δοῦλοι.
3. τὸ κέντρον λαμβάνουσι καὶ βραδέως προσχωροῦσι τοῖς βουσίν.
4. σπεύδετε, ὦ βόες· μὴ ἐν τῷ ἀγρῷ καθεύδετε.
5. οὐ δυνατόν ἐστι τοὺς βοῦς ἐξελαύνειν· ἰσχῡροὶ γάρ εἰσιν.

In these sentences students are expected to produce forms that have not yet been given in the grammar sections (e.g., οἱ βόες, τοὺς βοῦς, and ὦ βόες), but they have seen examples of these very phrases in passage α and Exercise 3b; if they hesitate in writing them, they should be encouraged to check back in the reading and Exercise 3b and locate examples. Likewise, the preposition ἐν has not been formally introduced in a vocabulary list, but students have met examples (including ἐν τῷ ἀγρῷ, passage 1β:1) and should be aware by now that this preposition is followed by the dative case.

The Deme and the Polis

Be sure to have students mark an appropriate location of Cholleidae on the map, about twelve miles southeast of Athens.

For further reading, see *The World of Athens*, p. 69 and pp. 73–78, and *The Oxford History of the Classical World*, pp. 207–210.

Ο ΑΡΟΤΟΣ (β)

Illustration

See note on illustration for 3α (see above, page 12).

Caption under Illustration

"It is not possible, master, to carry out so many stones": students will find the meaning of τοσούτους in the vocabulary list.

Vocabulary

With this vocabulary and reading we begin to introduce third declension nouns. Along with each third declension noun in the vocabulary list we give the forms that appear in the reading, with the definite articles or the ὦ-marker for vocatives, which will serve to identify the forms for students.

Translation

Lines 1–5

Meanwhile Philip approaches; Philip is Dicaeopolis's son, a big and brave boy (a boy both big and brave); (and) he is bringing (the) dinner to his father. And when he enters (into) the field, he calls his father and says, "Come here, father; look! I am bringing dinner. And so no longer work but sit and eat."

[Compound verb to be deduced: εἰσβαίνει (3).

Word glossed earlier in chapter: ἰδού look!]

Lines 6–16

And so the father leaves the plow and calls the slave. And so they sit together and eat. But after dinner Dicaeopolis says, "Stay, boy, and help. Take the seed and sow it in the ground. And you, Xanthias, dig (up) the stones and carry (them) out of the field. For the stones are many and it is scarcely possible to plow." But Xanthias says, "But it is not possible to carry out so many stones." But Dicaeopolis (says), "Don't talk nonsense, Xanthias, but work." And so the father and the son and the slave work. But at last the sun sets, and the men no longer work but loosen the oxen, and they leave the plow in the field and walk slowly toward the house.

[Words glossed earlier in chapter: ἅμα together   τὸ σπέρμα the seed σπεῖρε sow   φλυᾱρεῖ talk nonsense.]

Word Building

1. I fall into,
2. I fall out (of)
3. I lead into
4. I lead to(ward)
5. I look toward

Grammar 2

Emphasize the two rules for the neuter: (1) accusative = nominative and (2) nominative and accusative plural end in α.

Exercise 3d

1. τούς 2. οἱ 3. τοῖς 4. τῶν 5. τά 6. τῶν 7. τό 8. τόν 9. οἱ 10. τούς

Exercise 3e

1. οἱ δοῦλοι πονοῦσιν ἐν τοῖς ἀγροῖς.
   The slaves work in the fields.
2. οἱ ἄνθρωποι σπεύδουσι πρὸς τὸν οἶκον.
   The men hurry toward the house.
3. ὅ τε Δικαιόπολις καὶ ὁ δοῦλος μένουσιν ἐν τῷ ἀγρῷ.
   Dicaeopolis and the slave remain in the field.
4. λείπετε τὰ ἄροτρα, ὦ δοῦλοι, ἐν τῷ ἀγρῷ.
   Leave the plows in the field, slaves.
5. αἴρετε τοὺς λίθους, ὦ δοῦλοι, καὶ ἐκφέρετε ἐκ τῶν ἀγρῶν.
   Lift the stones, slaves, and carry (them) out of the fields.
6. οὐ δυνατόν ἐστι τοὺς λίθους αἴρειν καὶ ἐκφέρειν.
   It is not possible to lift the stones and carry (them) out.

This type of exercise gives good practice with endings. Teachers can easily generate more exercises of this sort, using sentences from the readings or from other exercises as raw material.

Exercise 3f

1. Dicaeopolis drives the oxen, but the oxen no longer drag the plow.
   ὁ μὲν δεσπότης καλεῖ τοὺς δούλους, οἱ δὲ δοῦλοι οὐκ ἐλαύνουσι τοὺς βοῦς.
2. Don't sit in the house, boys, but come here and help.
   μὴ μένετε ἐν τοῖς ἀγροῖς, ὦ παῖδες, ἀλλὰ βαδίζετε πρὸς τὸν οἶκον καὶ καθεύδετε.

3. The boys are strong, for they are
    carrying big stones.
    οἱ δοῦλοι ῥᾴθυμοί εἰσιν· οὐκέτι γὰρ
    πονοῦσιν.
4. Take the plows, friends, and hurry
    to the fields.
    λύετε τοὺς βοῦς, ὦ δοῦλοι, καὶ
    λείπετε τὰ ἄροτρα ἐν τῷ ἀγρῷ.
5. Why are you fleeing, boys? Be
    brave.
    διὰ τί μένετε, ὦ παῖδες; μὴ ῥᾴθυμοι
    ἔστε.

The first sentence of the pair in no. 2
introduces the vocative plural of the third
declension noun παῖς, and that form is
required in the corresponding English to
Greek sentence. The nominative plural
occurs in no. 3 (with the definite article
as a gender-number-case indicator),
and the vocative plural again in no. 5.
In no. 3 students are to deduce μεγάλους
from μέγας, which they had in passage α.
Students should remember φίλοι =
"friends" (no. 4) from the Word
Building in Chapter 1, page 9. In no. 5,
we use the second person plural
indicative φεύγετε (glossed), which will
be formally presented in Chapter 4.
Students encountered one second person
plural indicative form, μένετε, in 3α:5.
In the English to Greek sentence no. 5,
students are to reproduce the ending
found in φεύγετε.

ΟΙ ΒΟΕΣ

Title: "The Oxen"

Translation

Lines 1–8
Both the master and the slave are
walking to the field. The slave carries
the plow; the master drives the oxen. But
when they approach the field, the oxen go

no longer. And so the master calls them
and says, "Don't wait/Don't be idle,
oxen, but hurry into the field." But the
oxen are still waiting/idle. And so the
master calls the slave and says, "Come
here, Xanthias, and help. For the oxen
are waiting/idle and it is not possible to
drive them into the field." And so the
slave approaches and says, "But it is
possible, look!" and he goads the oxen.
And they are no longer waiting/idle but
hurry into the field.
[Word glossed earlier in chapter: ἰδού
look!]

Exercise 3g

1. ὁ δεσπότης εἰς τὸν ἀγρὸν σπεύδει.
2. βλέπει πρὸς τὸν ἀγρὸν καί,
    "τοσοῦτοι," φησίν, "λίθοι εἰσὶν ἐν τῷ
    ἀγρῷ. οὐ δυνατόν ἐστιν ἀροτρεύειν.
    ἐλθὲ δεῦρο, ὦ δοῦλε, καὶ ἔκφερε τοὺς
    λίθους ἐκ τοῦ ἀγροῦ."
3. ὁ δὲ δοῦλος, "οὐ δυνατόν ἐστιν,"
    φησίν, "τοσούτους λίθους ἐκφέρειν
    ἐκ τοῦ ἀγροῦ. σὺ οὖν βοήθει.

Remind students in doing nos. 2
and 3 that φησί(ν), used with quoted
words, is postpositive and always placed
parenthetically in the middle of the
quoted words or after them.
Also in nos. 2 and 3, remind students that redundancy is proper and effective: "carry the stones out of the field"
= ἔκφερε . . . ἐκ. . . . Use of the uncompounded verb would, however, be quite
acceptable.
In no. 3, note that σύ is expressed,
since it is emphatic (note the italics in
the student's book), and that οὖν is used
to connect the last sentence with the previous words, although no such connecting word appears in English.

4
ΠΡΟΣ ΤΗΙ ΚΡΗΝΗΙ (α)

Title: "By the Spring"

Encourage students to deduce the meaning of the title from the picture before locating the words in the vocabulary list.

The purposes of this chapter are:

1. Reading: (α and β) to introduce Dicaeopolis's wife, Myrrhine, and daughter, Melissa, to show them engaged in an activity typical for females in the Greek world (fetching water from the spring), and to introduce a new strand of the plot (a trip to Athens to take part in a festival) that will develop in later chapters
2. Grammar: (α) to complete the presentation of singular and plural verb forms with the 1st and 2nd persons plural and to introduce first declension feminine nouns in all cases, singular and plural, with distinctions between those ending in -η, -ᾱ, and -ᾰ; (β) to present the forms of masculine nouns of the first declension, to consolidate the forms of first and second declension adjectives, to present the forms of μέγας and πολύς, which are mostly those of first and second declension adjectives, to introduce the formation of adverbs, and to consolidate the forms of the definite article and to stress its usefulness as a case indicator
3. Background: to present a discussion of the life of women in the Greek world

Illustration

Drawn from an Attic black figure hydria in the manner of the Antimenes Painter, ca. 480 B.C. (London, British Museum).

Caption under Illustration

"The girls are filling their water jars by the spring." Use comprehension questions in English to get the students to deduce the meaning of the Greek. "Where are the girls?" "What do the girls have?" "What are they doing with them?"

The caption introduces first declension nouns in three cases; similarities to the second declension masculine nouns that the students have already learned may be pointed out: -ι in the nominative plural, -ς in the accusative plural, and ι subscript in the dative singular.

Note that the contract verb πληρόω is used a number of times in this chapter. It is glossed in the reading passages; it is not intended that students learn the forms of the -o- contract verbs at this stage in the course (they are given in Chapter 15). The verb πληρόω is used in this chapter simply as a glossed vocabulary item.

Vocabulary

The verb ἐθέλω means "to be willing" in the sense of "to consent." It may be contrasted with βούλομαι, which will be introduced in Chapter 6 and means "I want." Both verbs may mean "to wish."

The phrase οὐκ ἐθέλω may often best be translated "I refuse," but sometimes a milder "I do not wish" may fit the context better.

Students should be alerted to the fact that some adjectives have only two terminations, such as ῥάθῡμος, ῥάθῡμον. This is a good opportunity to compare with φίλος, φίλη, φίλον just below. Cf. 2β:14 ἵλαος ἴσθι.

Translation

Lines 1–9
And the next day when the sun first rises, the wife calls her husband and says, "Get up, husband; for the sun is rising, and the slave is already leading the oxen to the field, and our daughter

and I (I and the daughter) intend to walk to the spring. Get up. It is time to go to the field." But Dicaeopolis is very tired and refuses (does not want) to get up (to raise himself); and so he says, "Don't be hard, wife; I am very tired and want to sleep." But his wife says, "But it is not possible to go on sleeping (still to sleep); for it is time to work. Get up, you lazy man."

[This may be a good time to begin asking some questions in Greek as the passage is read in class, e.g., δία τί ὁ Δικαιόπολις ἐθέλει καθεύδειν; Answer: ὁ Δικαιόπολις ἐθέλει καθεύδειν ὅτι μάλα κάμνει.

A number of reflexive pronouns occur in this passage; treat them as vocabulary items at this stage.

Note that it is normal Greek to say ἐγὼ δὲ καὶ ἡ θυγάτηρ "I and the (our) daughter" (3), whereas in normal, polite English we put the first person pronoun last: "our daughter and I." Greek puts first that which is of primary importance to the speaker.

ἐν νῷ ἔχομεν (4): students will deduce the new 1st person plural form from the subjects of the verb (ἐγὼ καὶ ἡ θυγάτηρ). Other 1st person plural forms will be met in the third paragraph, where the context makes the meaning clear.]

Lines 10–14

And so Dicaeopolis gets up reluctantly (with difficulty) and walks to the field, and Myrrhine and Melissa are walking to the spring (Melissa is the daughter, a very beautiful girl). And so both the mother and daughter go slowly; for they are carrying the water jars; and the water jars are big, so that it is not possible to hurry.

Lines 15–22

But when they approach the spring, look! other women are already there and are filling their water jars. And so Myrrhine calls the women and says, "Greetings, friends; are you already filling your jars?" And they say, "Greetings to you, too; yes, we are already filling our jars; for we've got here

(we are present) early. But come here quickly and listen; (for) a messenger has come from the city, and he says that the Athenians are holding (making) a festival. And so we intend to go to the city; for we want to see the dances and the competitions. Do you too want to see the festival?"

[This paragraph introduces 1st and 2nd person plural verbs: χαίρετε (17), πληροῦτε (17), πληροῦμεν (18), πάρεσμεν (19), ἔχομεν (21), and ἐθέλομεν (21); after students have studied the plural verb forms in the following grammar section, they will be asked to locate the 1st and 2nd person plural verb forms in the reading.

"χαῖρε καὶ σύ" (18): students may need to be reminded that καί can mean "too" ("you too"). Grammatically, σύ emphasizes the subject of the imperative χαῖρε.

Students have seen the adjective Ἀθηναῖος before, and they should deduce οἱ Ἀθηναῖοι (20) as "the Athenians" without trouble. It may be commented that adjectives may be used as substantives with the definite article.

ἑορτὴν ποιοῦσιν (20): "are holding/celebrating (literally, making) a festival." Students should be warned that some words such a ποιέω are used in a wide variety of idiomatic expressions and that they will need to find the right English translation.]

Word Study

1. *acoustics* (1683): ἀκούω, ἀκουστικός, -ή, -όν = "concerned with hearing." Aristotle, *De anima* 426e has τὰ ἀκουστικά "the faculty of hearing," but the English word means the whole science of the phenomenon of hearing.

2. *angel*: ὁ ἄγγελος "the messenger (of God)."

3. *gynecology* (coined, 1847): ἡ γυνή, τῆς γυναικός + ὁ λόγος, -λογίᾱ = "the branch of medicine dealing with diseases peculiar to women."

4. *choreographer* (coined, 1876): ὁ
χόρος + γράφω, ὁ γραφεύς "drawer,
writer" = one who designs dances.

5. *tachometer* (coined, 1810): ταχέως, τὸ
τάχος "speed" + τὸ μέτρον
"measurement" = "an instrument
for measuring speed."

6. *philanthropist*: φιλάνθρωπ-ος, -ον
(φιλ-έω + ὁ ἄνθρωπος) + -ist.

7. *polyandry*: ἡ πολυανδρίᾱ (πολύς +
ἀνέρ, ἀνδρ-ός) = "populousness,"
but in English = the form of
polygamy in which one woman has
many husbands.

8. *misogynist*: ὁ μῑσογύνης, -ου (μῑσέω
"I hate" + ἡ γυνή + ist) = "a hater of
women."

Grammar 1

Note that space does not allow us to
give translations of verb forms; the
teacher should be sure that students can
translate each form, e.g., "I loosen," "I
am loosening," "I do loosen," etc.

Exercise 4a

ἔχομεν (4), πληροῦτε (17), πληροῦμεν
(18), πάρεσμεν (19), ἔχομεν (21), and
ἐθέλομεν (21)

Grammar 2

Note that in the paradigms of nouns
and adjectives that end in α, we include
the macron over the dative singular with
its iota subscript to avoid the odd appear-
ance of having macrons over other alphas in the singular and not over the dative. Alphas with iota subscript are always long; and so are normally not
marked with macrons.

Exercise 4b

1. τῆς Μυρρίνης
2. τῆς Μελίττης
3. τῆς καλῆς οἰκίας
4. τῆς καλῆς ἑορτῆς
5. τῆς καλῆς κρήνης
6. τοῦ μακροῦ πόνου
7. τῆς μῑκρᾶς θαλάττης
8. τοῦ καλοῦ δένδρου

Exercise 4c

1. αἱ 2. τῷ 3. τῇ 4. τῶν 5. τῆς 6. ταῖς
7. τὰ 8. οἱ

Exercise 4d

1. αἱ κόραι ἄγουσι τὰς φίλᾱς ἐκ τῶν
ἀγρῶν.
The girls lead their friends out of the
fields.

2. αἱ δοῦλαι τὰς ὑδρίᾱς φέρουσι πρὸς
τὰς κρήνᾱς.
The slaves are carrying the water
jars to the springs.

3. καλαί εἰσιν αἱ κόραι· ἆρ' οὐκ ἐθέ-
λετε αὐτὰς καλεῖν;
The girls are beautiful; don't you
wish to call them?

4. χαίρετε, ὦ κόραι· ἆρα βαδίζετε πρὸς
τὰς οἰκίᾱς;
Greetings, girls! are you walking to
your homes?

5. ἐν νῷ ἔχομεν λείπειν τὰς ὑδρίᾱς ἐν
ταῖς οἰκίαις καὶ βοηθεῖν.
We intend to leave the water jars in
the houses and help.

Exercise 4e

1. ἡ φίλη μένει πρὸς τῇ κρήνῃ.
The friend is waiting by the spring.

2. ὁ ἄνθρωπος φέρει τὸ ἄροτρον ἐκ τοῦ
ἀγροῦ.
The man is carrying the plow out of
the field.

3. ἄκουε, ὦ φίλε· ἐν νῷ ἔχω βαδίζειν
πρὸς τὴν οἰκίᾱν.
Listen, friend, I intend to go to the
house.

4. τί ποιεῖς, ὦ δοῦλε; μὴ οὕτω σκαιὸς
ἴσθι.
What are you doing, slave? Don't be
so clumsy.

Women

Illustration (page 35)

Interior of Attic red figure cylix, ca.
450 B.C., Painter of Bologna (New York,
Metropolitan Museum).

For further reading, see *The World
of Athens*, pp. 147–149 and 162–171, and

The Oxford History of the Classical World, pp. 210–217.

ΠΡΟΣ ΤΗΙ ΚΡΗΝΗΙ (β)

Caption under Illustration

"Melissa says, 'It's not my fault (I am not to blame); (for) the water jar is big.'"

Vocabulary

Point out the second declension feminine noun ἡ ὁδός; see Chapter 5, Grammar 8, p. 52.

Paradigms of adjectives, are given in Grammar 4 in this chapter.

Translation

Lines 1–4

But Myrrhine (says), "What are you saying, friends? Are the Athenians really holding a festival? I very much want to see it; and you, Melissa, do you too want to see (it)? But it's not possible; for my husband is hard; for he is always working and is rarely willing to go to the city."

["But Myrrhine (says)" (1): Greek sometimes omits "says" before quotations.

Words glossed earlier in chapter: θεωρεῖν to see   τὸ ἄστυ the city.]

Lines 5–7

But Melissa says, "But father is not very hard; it is easy to persuade him." And Myrrhine says, "Don't talk such nonsense, but fill your jar quickly. For it is time to return home."

Lines 8–13

And so both mother and daughter quickly fill their jars and walk home. But on the way Melissa stumbles and drops the jar on the ground and breaks it. And so she groans and says, "Alas! It's not my fault (I am not to blame); for the jar is big, and it is not possible to carry it." But her mother says,"What are you saying, daughter? Don't talk nonsense, but hurry home and bring another water jar."

[Words glossed earlier in chapter: πληροῦσι are filling   μεγάλη big.]

Lines 14–15

And so Melissa hurries home, and Myrrhine walks slowly, for the jar is big and she does not want to drop it.

Word Building

This set illustrates the formation of verbs from noun stems by adding the suffix -ευω. Such verbs indicate a state or activity.
1. dance; I dance
2. slave; I am a slave
3. plow; I plow
4. horse; I am a horseman, I ride

Grammar 3

The recessive accent of the vocative δέσποτα is irregular; compare πολῖτα (from ὁ πολίτης).

Grammar 4

Call the following rules to the attention of students: (1) the accent of adjectives is persistent, i.e., it stays where it is in the nom. masc. sing. unless forced to move, (2) adjectives with an acute accent on the ultima circumflex the genitive and dative singular and plural, and (3) unlike nouns of the first declension, these adjectives do not circumflex the ultima of the genitive plural (e.g., ῥᾳδίων) unless the accent is already on the ultima (e.g., καλῶν).

Grammar 5

Notes:

Grammar 6

Notes:

Exercise 4f

ἀληθῶς (1), σπανίως (4), ταχέως (7, 8), and βραδέως (14).

Exercise 4g

1. acc. pl. 2. dat. sing. 3. dat. sing. 4. acc. sing. 5. voc. sing. 6. acc. sing. 7. gen. sing. 8. gen. sing. 9. dat. pl. 10. gen. sing. 11. nom. pl. 12. gen. sing. 13. dat. pl. 14. acc. sing. 15. voc. sing.

ΑΙ ΓΥΝΑΙΚΕΣ ΤΟΥΣ ΑΝΔΡΑΣ ΠΕΙΘΟΥΣΙΝ

Title: "The Women Persuade Their Husbands"

Translation

Lines 1–9

Many women have come to the spring. While they are filling their jars, a messenger approaches. And when he is there, he says, "Listen, women; (for) the Athenians are holding a festival. Don't you want to see it? And so persuade your husbands to take you there." And the women rejoice and say, "We very much want to see (it), and we intend to persuade our husbands." And so they quickly fill their jars and hurry home. And when their husbands have come from the fields, each wife says, "Listen, dear husband; a messenger is here and says that the Athenians are holding a festival. Won't you (are you not willing to) take me there?" And they easily persuade them; for the husbands themselves want to see the festival.

[Remind students that εἰς (1) can mean "to" as well as "into."

Words glossed earlier in chapter: **ἥκουσιν** have come **πληροῦσι** are filling **αὐτήν** it **θεωρεῖν** to see.

Note the predicate position of the adjective in the phrase ἑκάστη ἡ γυνή (6–7): let the students simply translate "each woman"; the phrase need not be analyzed at this stage.]

Illustration (page 41)

Detail of Attic black figure lekythos by the Amasis Painter, ca. 560 B.C. (New York, Metropolitan Museum).

Exercise 4h

1. ὁ Δικαιόπολις τῇ Μυρρίνῃ προσχωρεῖ καί, "χαῖρε, φίλη γύναι," φησίν, "τί ποιεῖς;"
2. "ἐγὼ πρὸς τὴν κρήνην σπεύδω. ἐθέλω γὰρ φέρειν τὸ ὕδωρ πρὸς τὴν οἰκίᾱν (τὸν οἶκον). σὺ δὲ τί ποιεῖς;"
3. "ἐγώ τε καὶ ὁ δοῦλος πρὸς τὸν ἀγρὸν σπεύδομεν. ἀλλ' ἄκουε.
4. "οἱ γὰρ Ἀθηναῖοι ἑορτὴν ποιοῦσιν. ἆρ' ἐθέλεις αὐτὴν θεωρεῖν;"
5. "ἐγὼ μάλιστα ἐθέλω θεωρεῖν. μὴ οὖν πρὸς τὸν ἀγρὸν ἴθι ἀλλὰ ἄγε με πρὸς τὸ ἄστυ."

In no. 2 the pronouns *I* and *you* are emphatic and so are expressed: ἐγώ . . . σὺ δέ. Note also that Greek has δέ after σύ since there is a change of subject.

In no. 3 students should reverse the polite order of the subjects in the English and put the 1st person pronoun first in their Greek.

The elisions in nos. 3 and 4 are optional, but students should become accustomed to writing with elisions.

Students may need to be reminded of the idiom for "holding a festival" in no. 4 (ἑορτὴν ποιεῖν); see line 20 in the last paragraph in passage α at the beginning of this chapter.

5
Ο ΛΥΚΟΣ (α)

Title: "The Wolf"

Students will find the word in the vocabulary list.

The purposes of this chapter are:

1. Reading: (α and β) to introduce Philip's grandfather and Philip's dog Argus into the story, to relate an incident involving first pursuit of a hare and then Philip's slaying of a wolf, and finally to make a transition to narration of the myth of Theseus and the Minotaur
2. Grammar: (α) to present the forms of contract verbs in -α-, to note that neuter plural subjects take singular verbs, and to observe the pronominal use of the article + δέ at the beginning of a clause; (β) to present full sets of the personal pronouns and the adjective/pronoun αὐτός, to present the possessive adjectives and the use of the genitive of αὐτός to show possession, to clarify the distinction between attributive and predicate position, and to note that some nouns of the second declension are feminine
3. Background: to present some background information on Greek religion

Caption under Illustration

"Philip sees a hare in the field, and he shouts, "Go on, Argus! Chase (it)": the new words are given in the vocabulary list. Note that δή is used to emphasize the preceding word, ἴθι. Be sure students understand the distinction between a hare and a rabbit (see any English dictionary).

Vocabulary

ἄπειμι: compare πάρειμι (see Vocabulary 2α).

We introduce the imperatives ἴθι and ἴτε here just as we introduced ἐλθέ in Chapter 2. The infinitives ἰέναι and ἐπανιέναι will be introduced in the vocabulary lists in Chapters 7α and 9β respectively.

The word for "hare" is of the so-called Attic declension, which need not be formally presented to students. The word will appear only in the nominative and accusative singular, and students will be able to recognize the forms from the definite articles and from the familiar -ς and -ν endings. (For teacher reference only, we give the following set of forms: λαγώς, λαγώ, λαγῴ, λαγών; λαγῴ, λαγών, λαγῴς, λαγώς.)

For the difference between ἡ οἰκίᾱ and ὁ οἶκος, see notes to Chapter 6, Word Building, page 33 in this handbook.

Κατά is first used as a preposition in the reading at the end of this chapter, but it is used as a prefix in καταβαίνω and καταπίπτω in passages α and β, where students are expected to deduce the meanings of the compound verbs.

The conjunction ὥστε introduces two types of result clauses, one with the indicative (*actual result*, describing something that actually happens, as in lines 8–9 of passage α) and the other with the infinitive (*natural result*, describing a general tendency, as in 9β:20). Discussion of this distinction may be postponed until students have met a number of examples.

Some students will recognize the name of the dog, Argus, as that of Odysseus' dog. The related adjective ἀργός has two distinct but interrelated meanings, "shining" and "swift" (compare our combination of these notions in the phrase "silver streak"), and dogs are frequently referred to as ἀργοί, "swift."

Translation

Lines 1–9

While Myrrhine and Melissa are away, grandfather is working in the garden, and the boy and Argus are walking to the sheepfold; Argus is a dog, big and strong; he guards the house and the flocks. When (both) the boy and the dog are walking up the road, Philip sees a hare in the field; and so he looses the dog and says, "Go on, Argus! Chase (it)." And so Argus barks and chases the hare, and the hare flees up the hill. And they run so quickly that soon it is not possible to see either the dog or the hare.

[Students should easily be able to deduce the meaning of the forms of the -α- contract verbs: ὁρᾷ (5) and ὁρᾶν (8) in the first paragraph, βοᾷ (10), ὁρᾷ (12), and βοᾷ (12) in the second paragraph, and ὁρᾷ (15) and βοῶ (20) in the third paragraph.

In lines 8–9, note that οὐ δυνατόν ἐστιν ὁρᾶν οὔτε τὸν κύνα οὔτε τὸν λαγών = (literally) "it is not possible to see neither the dog nor the hare"; Greek often doubles its negatives for emphasis, while English does not.]

Lines 10–14

And so Philip hurries after them and shouts, "Come here, Argus. Come back, you cursed dog." But the dog still chases (the hare). And so Philip runs to the top of the hill, but he does not see the dog. And so he shouts loudly and calls, but Argus does not hear. Finally the boy despairs and comes down the hill.

[Compound verb to be deduced (see Chapter 2, Word Building, page 17): κατα-βαίνει (14).]

Lines 15–22

But when he approaches the garden, grandfather sees him and says, "What are you doing, boy? Where have you come from and where is Argus?" And Philip says, "I have come from the sheepfold, grandpa. Argus is somewhere in the hills; for he is chasing a hare. But grandfather says, "Go on, boy! Why aren't you looking for him? Don't be so lazy." And Philip says, "I'm not lazy, grandpa, and it's not my fault (nor am I to blame). For I shout loudly and call (him), but the dog doesn't hear." And grandfather says, "Come here, boy. So he says and takes his stick and hurries up the road together with the boy.

Word Study

1. *geology* (coined, 1735): γῆ + λόγος, -λογίᾱ = "study of the earth."
2. *geography*: γῆ + γράφω, ἡ γραφή = ἡ γεωγραφίᾱ = "drawing, description of the earth."
3. *geometry*: ἡ γῆ + τὸ μέτρον = γεωμετρίᾱ "measurement of the land," "land surveying," "geometry."
4. *geocentric*: ἡ γῆ + τὸ κέντρον = "earth at the center." See on *heliocentric*, Chapter 2, Word Study, no. 3.

Note that in these compounds γῆ is shortened to γε and ω is inserted; your students met in Chapter 1, Word Building, no. 3, the word γεωργός = a land (γε-) worker (εργ-) or farmer (cf. English *George*).

It is said that Greek mathematicians developed geometry from a study of the Egyptian system of surveying land; e.g., the Egyptians knew in practice that the square on the hypotenuse of a triangle with sides 3, 4, and 5 was equivalent in area to the sum of the squares on the other two sides; Pythagoras (floruit 530 B.C.) stated the general theory implied by this fact.

Grammar 1

Notes:

Exercise 5a

ὁρᾷ (5), ὁρᾶν (8), βοᾷ (10), ὁρᾷ, βοᾷ (12), ὁρᾷ (15), and βοῶ (20).

Grammar 2

Neuter plural subjects are regarded as collectives (with endings related to the -ᾱ ending of the stem of first declension nouns) and therefore regularly take singular verbs.

Grammar 3

Notes:

Exercise 5b

1. honor! *or* you honor τίμᾱ/τῑμᾷς
2. they love φιλεῖ
3. we see ὁρῶ
4. live! *or* you live οἴκει/οἰκεῖς
5. we do/make ποιῶ
6. they are shouting βοᾷ
7. see! *or* you see ὅρα/ὁρᾷς
8. they are working πονεῖ

Exercise 5c

1. he honors τῑμῶσιν(ν)
2. you love φιλεῖτε
3. I seek ζητοῦμεν
4. I see ὁρῶμεν
5. you are shouting βοᾶτε
6. he is living οἰκοῦσι(ν)
7. love! φιλεῖτε
8. honor! τῑμᾶτε

Exercise 5d

1. The dog sees the hare and chases (it) to the top of the hill.
   ὁ πατὴρ μέγα βοᾷ καὶ τὸν δοῦλον ἐκ τῆς οἰκίας (ἐκ)καλεῖ.
2. Do you see the hare? Why don't you loose the dog?
   τί ποιεῖτε, ὦ φίλοι; διὰ τί σῑγᾶτε;
3. The man is so deaf that we always shout loudly.
   ὁ παῖς οὕτω ἀνδρεῖός ἐστιν ὥστε μέγα τῑμῶμεν αὐτόν.
4. We intend to walk to the city and see the dances.
   ἐθέλομεν πρὸς τὸ ἱερὸν βαδίζειν καὶ τὸν θεὸν τῑμᾶν.

5. Don't be so lazy, boy; go to the hill and look for the dog.
   μὴ οὕτω χαλεπὸς ἴσθι, ὦ πάππε. οὐ γὰρ αἴτιός εἰμι ἐγώ.

The following word glossed in passage α is needed in this exercise: μέγα "loudly."

Grammar 4

Note that elision between words is not obligatory in Greek prose and will not always occur in the readings and exercises in this book. The practice of Greek authors varies considerably.

Gods and Men

Illustration

Bronze statue from a shipwreck off Artemisium (north Euboea), ca. 460 B.C. (Athens, National Archaeological Museum).

For further reading, see *The World of Athens*, pp. 89–131, and *The Oxford History of the Classical World*, Chapter 11, "Greek Religion," pp. 254–274.

Ο ΛΥΚΟΣ (β)

Caption under Illustration

"Argus rushes at the wolf": students will recognize the form of the verb; encourage them to deduce its meaning and the meaning of the prepositional phrase from the illustration.

Vocabulary

The verb πάσχω is often translated freely to suit the context. For example, τί πάσχεις, literally, "What are you suffering?" may better be rendered "What is wrong with you?" or "What is happening to you?"

This vocabulary list contains pronouns (ἡμεῖς, ὑμεῖς) and the intensive adjective/pronoun αὐτός, which are treated in Grammar 5 and must be learned thoroughly. Students have met some forms of αὐτός used as a 3rd person pronoun, and the form αὐτήν "her" occurs in line 21 of the following reading passage.

Translation

Lines 1–9

But when Philip and his grandfather approach the sheepfold, they hear a lot of (much) noise; for Argus is barking savagely and the flocks are making a great uproar. And so they hurry; for they want to learn what is the matter with the flocks (what the flocks are suffering). And so the boy is there first and look! Argus is staying by the road and barking savagely, and down from the hill toward the sheepfold comes a great wolf. And so Philip shouts loudly and takes stones and pelts the wolf; and Argus rushes at it and falls on (it) so fiercely that the wolf turns back and flees away. And so the dog chases (it), and Philip hurries after him.

[Note that ἀναστρέφει (8) may be used intransitively, as here.

Compound verb to be deduced: ἀποφεύγει (9).

Words glossed earlier in chapter: τῷ αὐλίῳ the sheepfold ὑλακτεῖ barks.]

Lines 10–14

Now grandfather has come to the top of the hill and sees the wolf and shouts, "Come here, Philip; don't chase (the wolf) but come back." But now Argus seizes the wolf and holds it with his teeth, and Philip is already there and takes his knife and strikes the wolf. And it shudders and falls to the ground.

[Word glossed earlier in chapter: ἐπάνελθε come back!

Compound verb to be deduced: καταπίπτει (14).]

Lines 15–19

At that very moment grandfather approaches and sees the wolf lying on the ground. And so he is amazed and says, "Well done, boy; you are very brave.

For it is a big wolf and fierce. And you, Argus, are a good dog; for you guard the flocks well. But now, Philip, hurry home; for your mother, I suppose, wishes to learn where you are and what is happening to you (what you are suffering, experiencing)."

[ἐνταῦθα δή (15): the word ἐνταῦθα is used of time to mean "then" and is frequently followed by δή, which emphasizes it, thus, "at that very moment."

ἐπὶ τῇ γῇ (15): ἐπί + dative = "on the ground"; compare ὁρμᾷ ἐπ’ αὐτόν "rushes at (against) it" in lines 7–8.]

Lines 20–26

And when they approach the house, they see mother. And so grandfather hurries to her and tells everything. And she says, "Are you telling the truth? Well done, son; you are very brave. But look! Melissa is coming from the spring. Come here, Melissa, and listen; (for) Philip has killed a wolf." And so grandfather tells everything again, and Melissa is very amazed and says that both Argus and Philip are very brave and strong.

[In line 25, the conjunctions καί . . . καί . . . (καὶ ὁ Ἄργος καὶ ὁ Φίλιππος) are used rather than τε . . . καί for emphasis, in a context where we would say "both . . . and . . ."]

Lines 26–29

Then mother says, "Now come here, dear (boy), and sit with us under the tree; for you are very tired. And you, Melissa, *you* sit down too. So listen; for I wish to tell you a beautiful story."

Lines 30–32

And so grandfather goes to sleep— for he is very tired—and the children sit under the tree and listen; for they wish to hear the story.

Word Building

The right-hand member of each set is a first declension feminine noun formed from the same root as a verb:
1. I shout; a shout
2. I honor; honor

3. I rush; rush, attack
4. I conquer; victory
5. I finish; end

Grammar 5

Notes:

Exercise 5e

Story α in Chapter 3: αὐτό (6), αὐτόν (7, 12, 14, 16, 19), ἐγώ (21), αὐτόν (21, 24).
Story β in Chapter 5: αὐτόν (8, 9), σύ (17), αὐτήν (21), μοι (28), σύ (28, 29), ἐγώ (29).

Grammar 6

Students should learn to be able to recognize the possessive adjectives as presented in this section; they were not given in the vocabulary list because they do not occur in the reading. They are, in fact, fairly rare in actual usage.

Grammar 7

Notes:

Grammar 8

Notes:

Exercise 5f

1. Come here, boy; for our master calls us.
2. What are you doing, slaves? For I am calling you, but you do not listen.
3. Don't you hear me? Bring (to) me the plow.
4. But, master, we are bringing it to you now.
5. Sit with us, boy, and tell me what the matter is (what you are suffering, experiencing).

6. I am looking for my dog, father; but he is fleeing up the road and refuses (is not willing) to come back.
7. Cheer up, boy; for I hear its (the dog's) voice. And so look for him.
8. I see him on the top of the hill; look! now he is running toward us.
9. The wolf is savage and big, but the boy takes his knife and strikes it.
10. The grandfather is now there, and the boy takes his (the grandfather's) knife and kills the wolf.

Ο ΑΡΓΟΣ
ΤΑ ΜΗΛΑ ΣΩΙΖΕΙ

Title: "Argus Saves the Flocks"

The verb will be unfamiliar. Ask students to guess its meaning; come back to it after reading the passage and see who was right. It will be clear that the story involves Argus, the flocks, and his doing something with them as the object of his action. Let this be the context within which the story is read, and then fill in the meaning of the verb σῴζει upon completion of the story.

Translation

Lines 1–7
    (Both) Philip and his father are walking slowly up the road. For they are looking for the flocks. But when they come to the top of the hill, they see the flocks; for they are staying by the road and making a great uproar. And so Dicaeopolis says, "What's the matter with the flocks? Hurry down the road, boy, and learn why they are making such (so great) an uproar." And so Philip hurries down the road. But when he approaches the flocks, he sees a great wolf; and so he calls his father and shouts, "Come here, father, and help. For there's a great wolf here, and it is about to to attack the flocks."
[Word glossed earlier in chapter: θόρυβον uproar.]

Lines 8–12

And so Dicaeopolis looses the dog
and says, "Go on, Argus; chase the wolf;
and you, son, stay there." And so Philip
waits by the road, and Argus barks and
rushes so fiercely at the wolf that the wolf
runs away. And Philip and his father
run after them and shout and throw
stones. At that very moment they call the
dog and drive the flocks home.

[Words glossed earlier in chapter:
ὑλακτεῖ barks   **ὁρμᾷ** rushes
ἐνταῦθα δή at that very moment.]

Exercise 5g

1. νῦν οὐχ ὁρῶμεν πολλοὺς λύκους ἐν
   τοῖς ὄρεσιν, καὶ σπανίως εἰς τοὺς
   ἀργοὺς καταβαίνουσιν.

2. θαυμάζομεν οὖν ὅτι ὁ Φίλιππος
   λύκον ἀπέκτονεν.

3. ἀγαθός ἐστιν ὁ παῖς καὶ τὰ μῆλα εὖ
   φυλάττει, ἀλλ' οὐκ αἰεὶ τὰ ἀληθῆ
   λέγει.

4. ἐν νῷ οὖν ἔχομεν πρὸς τὸ ὄρος
   σπεύδειν καὶ ζητεῖν τὸν νεκρόν.

6
Ο ΜΥΘΟΣ (α)

Title: "The Story"

The purposes of this chapter are:

1. Reading: to introduce a mythological strand into the narrative with the telling of the myth of Theseus, the Minotaur, and Ariadne
2. Grammar: (α) to introduce the middle voice and deponent verbs; (β) to tabulate uses of the dative case that have been encountered in the readings, including its use with certain verbs; and (β) to review the use of prepositions with the genitive, dative, and accusative cases
3. Background: to provide an introduction to myth

Illustration

Adapted from a detail of the François Vase, an Attic black figure crater by Kleitias, ca. 570 B.C. (Florence, Museo Archeologico). The scene on the vase actually represents Theseus' return to Attica.

Caption under Illustration

"Theseus and his companions arrive at Crete": all of the new words in this caption are included in the vocabulary list at the beginning of the chapter; comprehension questions may be used, e.g., "What is happening?"

The caption illustrates a deponent verb with a middle voice ending, and it provides a good opportunity to alert students to this new feature of the language (treated formally in Grammar 1). It is not desirable to go into the full explanation of deponent verbs and the middle voice at this point, but it is sufficient to explain that some verbs have endings different from those studied in the previous chapters. These verbs can then be picked out in the vocabulary list, and

note may be taken of the letters -αι at the end of the verb in the caption and at the end of all of the deponent verbs in the vocabulary list. It will be useful to inform students that the 3rd person of these deponent verbs ends in -ται (singular) and -νται (plural); awareness of this will help with the reading passage.

Vocabulary

Note the use of ἀφικνέομαι with the preposition εἰς, meaning "I arrive at."

The verb βοηθέω was introduced in the vocabulary list in Chapter 2β, but we repeat it here with the additional note that it is used with the dative case.

The verb βούλομαι should be contrasted with ἐθέλω. The former is used in the sense of "want" (implying choice or preference) and the latter in the sense of "being willing" (implying consent). Both may mean "to wish." See note in this handbook on Vocabulary in Chapter 4α.

The uncompounded verb ἔρχομαι does not occur in reading α, but it will be used in the exercises; it is introduced here to show the origin of the compound ἀπέρχομαι.

Students may note a relationship between πείθω "I persuade," introduced in Vocabulary 4β, and the middle/passive form given here, πείθομαι (+ dat.), "I obey." The latter form really means "I am persuaded," "I am won over," and therefore "I obey," and it takes a dative of agent. It is not necessary to explain all of this to students at this stage, and it is better to treat πείθομαι simply as a deponent verb that has its object in the dative case.

Note may be taken of the conjugation of πλέω: πλέω, πλεῖς, πλεῖ, πλέομεν, πλεῖτε, πλέουσι(ν). Only forms in -εε and -εει are contracted in Attic Greek.

The verb σῴζω has an ι subscript whenever ζ follows the ω; otherwise not.

Students should be told that when φοβέομαι is used transitively ("I fear, am afraid of") its object is in the accusative case (students should be warned not to be misled by the English translation "afraid *of*").

Note that we use the preferred English spelling Knossos. Here and elsewhere in the spelling of Greek proper names, we follow the *American Heritage Dictionary*.

Translation

Lines 1–6

"Minos lives in Crete; and he is king of the island. And in Minos's house is the labyrinth; and there lives the Minotaur, a terrible beast, half-man and half-bull. And the Minotaur eats men. And so Minos compels the Athenians to send seven youths and seven girls each year to Crete and gives them to the Minotaur to eat.

[The indefinite adjective τις, τι is introduced in this reading, but it will not be formally presented in the grammar until Chapter 7 (Grammar 6 and 7). Treat it simply as a vocabulary item here in Chapter 6, where it is always glossed. There is no need to go into the gender, number, and case of the various instances of the word in Chapter 6, but if questions arise simply point out that the adjective in each instance agrees with the noun it modifies: first paragraph θηρίον τι δεινόν (3), second paragraph παῖς τις (7). The indefinite adjective may be translated "a," "an," or "a certain."]

Lines 7-12

"But in Athens Aegeus is king; and he has a child called Theseus. And when he first grows up, he pities his comrades and wants to help them. And so he approaches his father and says, 'Dear papa, I pity my comrades and want to save (them). And so send me to Crete with my comrades.' Aegeus is very afraid but nevertheless obeys him.

[Note the accent on ἔστι (7) when it stands first in its clause. The possessive dative is glossed here and will be discussed

with other uses of the dative case in the second part of this chapter.

Note the other verbs used with the dative case in this paragraph (also discussed in the second part of this chapter): βοηθεῖν αὐτοῖς (9), προσχωρεῖ . . . τῷ πατρί (9), and πείθεται αὐτῷ (12).

Students have seen the deponent verb ἀφικνοῦνται in the caption under the picture at the beginning of this chapter, and they have seen eight deponent verbs in the vocabulary list. They should be able to deduce the third person singular endings of βούλεται (9), φοβεῖται (12), and πείθεται (12) in this paragraph from the context in which these forms are used.]

Lines 13–17

"And so Theseus goes on board (into) the ship with his comrades and sails to Crete. And when they arrive at the island, the king and the queen and their daughter, called Ariadne, receive them and lead them toward Knossos (for so they call the city of Minos) and guard them in the prison.

[Encourage idiomatic English translations of expressions such as εἰς τὴν ναῦν εἰσβαίνει: "goes on board the ship" rather than "goes into the ship."

Students will recognize the 3rd person plural endings of ἀφικνοῦνται (14) and δέχονται (15) from the use of ἀφικνοῦνται in the caption under the picture at the beginning of this chapter.]

Lines 18–28

"But as soon as (when first) Ariadne sees Theseus, she loves him and wants to save him. And so when night falls (happens), she hurries to the prison and calls Theseus and says, 'Be quiet, Theseus. I, Ariadne, am here. I love you and want to save (you). Look—I am giving you this sword and this thread. And so don't be afraid but go bravely into the labyrinth and kill the Minotaur. And then flee with your comrades and hurry to the ship. For I intend to wait by the ship; for I want to escape from Crete and sail with you to Athens.' So she says

and quickly goes away to the city.
Theseus is very surprised, but he accepts
the sword and waits for day."

[The passage introduces a verb used with
the genitive case (ἐρᾷ αὐτοῦ, 18). This
usage will not be formally presented until Chapter 9, Grammar 3d, p. 109, and
the phrase here should be treated simply
as a vocabulary item. From the phrase
here students will automatically deduce
the meaning of ἐρῶ σοῦ in line 21.

Encourage students to be flexible in
their translation of γίγνομαι, e.g., ἐπεὶ
οὖν γίγνεται ἡ νύξ (19): not "and so
when night happens," but "and so when
night falls."

Compound verb to be deduced:
ἔκφευγε (24).

Note the dieresis on νηΐ (25) and be
sure that students understand that the
word is pronounced as two syllables.

Note that the verb μένω can be either
intransitive ("I stay," "I wait") or transitive ("I wait for"), in which case it
takes a direct object, e.g., μένει τὴν
ἡμέρᾱν (28).]

Word Study

1. *phobia:* students should see the same
   root here as in φοβέομαι (vocabulary
   list). Then show them ὁ φόβος
   "fear." There is no Greek word ἡ
   φοβίᾱ, but the combining form
   -φοβίᾱ did exist, as in ὑδροφοβίᾱ
   "hydrophobia" = "fear of water" =
   "rabies." The English word *phobia*
   comes (through late and new Latin)
   from that Greek combining form
   and is itself used as a combining
   form in many English words. A
   phobia is an irrational fear or hatred
   of something.
2. *acrophobia:* ἄκρος, -α, -ον "top
   (of)" + -φοβίᾱ = "fear of heights."
3. *agoraphobia:* ἡ ἀγορά "agora,"
   "city center," "market place" +
   -φοβίᾱ = "fear of open spaces."
4. *entomophobia:* τὰ ἔντομα "insects"
   + -φοβίᾱ = "fear of insects." Cf. *en-
   tomology.*

5. *triskaidekaphobia:* τρεισκαίδεκα
   "thirteen" + -φοβίᾱ = "fear of the
   number thirteen."
6. *Anglophobia:* the meaning will be
   obvious. Have students think of
   other *-phobia* words, e.g., *claustro-
   phobia* and *xenophobia.* For other
   examples, see *A Dictionary of English Words from Greek and Latin
   Roots,* pp. 95–96.

Grammar 1

Top of page 57: for the use of
ἐγείρομαι as middle (rather than passive) and meaning "I wake up," cf. the
use of the second aorist middle, e.g.,
ἔγρετο Ζεύς (*Iliad* 15.4) and ἐξηγρόμην,
Aristophanes, *Frogs* 51. For the meaning
of λύομαι = "I secure the release of
(someone)," "I ransom," cf. λῡσόμενός
τε θύγατρα φέρων τ᾽ ἀπερείσι᾽ ἄποινα
(*Iliad* 1.13).

Help students as necessary with
translation of the forms of λύομαι and
φιλοῦμαι in the paradigms on pages 57
and 58. The forms of φιλοῦμαι follow the
same rules for contraction that are given
in Chapter 4, Grammar 1, on page 32.

Exercise 6a

βούλεται (9), βούλομαι (10), φοβεῖται
(12), πείθεται (12), ἀφικνοῦνται (14),
δέχονται (15), βούλεται (19), γίγνεται
(19), βούλομαι (21), βούλομαι (25),
ἀπέρχεται (27), and δέχεται (28). For
translations of the sentences, see the
translation of the passage above.

Exercise 6b

Sets of forms of this sort are not provided
in this handbook; teachers should check
students' work carefully.

Exercise 6c

1. I wash the dog.
   We wash (ourselves).
2. The mother wakes the child.
   The child wakes up.
3. The master stops the slave from
   work.
   I stop (from) work.

4. The slave is lifting the stones.
   The slave wakes and gets (lifts)
   himself up.
5. The boys turn the wheel (or hoop).
   The slave turns to his master.

In no. 2 students should deduce
παῖδα as acc. sing. of παῖς on the basis of
the definite article.

Students have met the reflexive pronoun as used in No. 4 in the first paragraph of the first reading in Chaper 4
(e.g., line 6). Either αἴρω or ἐπαίρω can
be used with the reflexive pronoun to
mean "I get up." These verbs are not
used with this sense in the middle voice.

Exercise 6d

1. λῡόμεθα
2. βούλονται
3. δέχεσθε
4. φοβούμεθα
5. ἀφικνοῦνται
6. γιγνόμεθα

Exercise 6e

1. λύῃ
2. πείθομαι
3. βούλεται
4. ἀφικνῇ
5. φοβοῦμαι
6. ἀφικνεῖται

In no. 4 we give only the indicative,
since the imperative of this verb is not
likely to be used.

Exercise 6f

1. We want to walk home.
2. They are not afraid of you (they do
   not fear you).
3. You are becoming lazy, slave.
4. We arrive at Crete.
5. The king is receiving us.

Exercise 6g

1. βουλόμεθα μένειν.
2. οὐ φοβοῦμαί σε (ὑμᾶς).
3. εἰς τὴν νῆσον ἀφικνοῦνται.
4. μὴ φοβεῖσθε, ὦ φίλοι.
5. ῥᾴθῡμοι γίγνονται.

Myth

Illustration (page 59)

Detail from Attic red figure calyx-
crater by the Niobid Painter, ca. 450 B.C.
(London, British Museum). Athena is
about to put a garland on Pandora's
head.

Illustration (page 61)

The throne room in the palace of
Minos at Knossos (ca. 1450 B.C.).

For further reading, see *The World
of Athens*, pp. 91–97, and *The Oxford
History of the Classical World*, pp. 78–88.

Ο ΜΥΘΟΣ (β)

Illustration

Drawn from an Attic black figure
cup (the Rayet cup), ca. 540 B.C. (Paris,
Louvre). While Theseus grapples with
the Minotaur, his companions watch
aghast. Theseus has already struck a
deadly blow to the beast's neck, from
which springs a stream of blood. The
bird flying between his legs is probably
Athena in disguise, assisting Theseus
(cf. *Odyssey* 22.239–240, where Athena,
disguised as a swallow, sits on a roof
beam and watches Odysseus slaughter-
ing the suitors).

Caption under Illustration

"Theseus is not afraid but fights
bravely and kills the Minotaur": students have had all of the words except
μάχεται, which is in this vocabulary list.

Vocabulary

The verb ἐξέρχομαι may be used
with either the simple genitive or the
preposition ἐκ + the genitive. We use it
with the preposition.

The particles γε and δή emphasize
the word they follow and often need not be
translated but might be rendered by tone
of voice.

Translation

Lines 1–8

"And when day comes, Minos goes
to the prison and calls Theseus and his
comrades and leads them to the
labyrinth. And when they arrive, the
slaves open the double gates and drive
the Athenians in. Then they close the
gates and go away; for thus they provide
food for the Minotaur for many days.
And so his comrades are very frightened, but Theseus says, 'Don't be afraid,
friends, for I will save you. And so follow me bravely.' So he speaks and leads
them into the labyrinth.

[Words glossed earlier in chapter: τὸ
δεσμωτήριον the prison   τῷ
Μῑνωταύρῳ to the Minotaur.

Compound verb to be deduced:
εἰσελαύνουσιν (4).

Note the two verbs with the dative
case: ἕπεσθέ μοι (7) and ἡγεῖται αὐτοῖς
(8); also ἡγεῖται τοῖς ἑταίροις in the
fourth paragraph (27).]

Lines 9–17

"Theseus holds the thread in his left
hand, and in his right hand the sword,
and goes forward into the darkness. His
comrades are very frightened, but nevertheless they follow, for necessity holds
them. And so they go a long way, and
often they turn, and often they hear terrible sounds; for the Minotaur is pursu-
ing them in the darkness and roars very
terribly. At that very moment they hear
the sound of feet and smell the breath of
the beast, and look!—the Minotaur is
there in their way. It roars terribly and
rushes at Theseus.

[Words glossed earlier in chapter: τὸ
λίνον the thread   τὸ ξίφος the
sword   ὅμως nevertheless.

μακρὰν . . . ὁδὸν πορεύονται (11–
12): "they go a long way"; this use of the
accusative should not cause students any
trouble and needs no explanation at this
stage.

The middle form ὁρμᾶται is used at
the end of this paragraph with the same

sense as the active form ὁρμᾷ in the first
paragraph of reading 5β (line 7). Two
-α- contract verbs are used in this paragraph (βρῡχᾶται, 14, 16, and ὁρμᾶται, 17);
the forms (to be formally presented in
Chapter 8, Grammar 2) need not be discussed at this stage.]

Lines 18–25

"But Theseus is not afraid but fights
very bravely; for with his left hand he
takes hold of the head of the beast, and
with his right hand he strikes its chest.
And the Minotaur shrieks terribly and
falls to the ground. And when his comrades see the beast lying on the ground,
they rejoice and say, 'Theseus, how
brave you are! How we admire and
honor you! But now save us from the
labyrinth and lead us to the gates. For
the road is long and the darkness thick
(much), and we do not know the way.'

[λαμβάνεται τῆς κεφαλῆς (19): note the
use of the genitive with the verb in the
middle voice, meaning "takes hold of."]

Lines 26–33

"But Theseus is not afraid but takes
the thread—for thus he learns the way—
and leads his comrades to the gates.
And when they arrive, they cut through
the bolt and wait; for it is still day. But
when night falls, they go out of the
labyrinth and hurry to the ship. And
there they see Ariadne; for she is
waiting by the ship. And so they quickly
go on board and sail away toward
Athens. And so thus Theseus kills the
Minotaur and brings his comrades
safely to Athens (literally, "saves his
comrades to Athens")."

[Compound verb to be deduced:
ἀποπλέουσι (31).]

Lines 34–38

So Myrrhine ends her story, but
Melissa says, "And Ariadne, is she
happy? Does Theseus love her?" And
Myrrhine (replies), "No, Ariadne is not
happy, and Theseus does not love her."
And Melissa (asks), "Why doesn't
Theseus love her? What happens?" But

her mother says, "I do not wish to tell you that story *now*."

[Note how in the last line γε emphasizes the preceding word: "not *now*—some other time."]

Word Building

The pairs of masculine and feminine forms in nos. 1–4 are straightforward, and the meanings of the words at the right can be easily deduced by the students. It may be mentioned that ἡ θεός is also used to mean goddess.

In no. 4, the word ἡ ἑταίρᾱ may be used simply of a female companion, but it may also be used of a courtesan or call-girl.

In no. 5. the difference between ὁ οἶκος and ἡ οἰκίᾱ will not be apparent because it is a matter of a difference in usage and not a difference in gender. Both words have occurred in vocabulary lists (Chapters 1 and 5) with the meaning "house," "home," "dwelling." Both are used of the house as a physical structure; οἶκος is also used of one's household goods or property in a larger, legal sense. In a strictly legal sense οἰκίᾱ refers to the house itself as opposed to the property left to one's heirs, but it should be noted that οἰκίᾱ may also have a more abstract sense of "household" or "family," though οἶκος may also have this sense of "house," as in "the house of Atreus." The two words overlap in meaning.

Grammar 2

Students have met the following verbs that are used with the dative case: ἕπομαι, βοηθέω, ἡγέομαι, πείθομαι, and προσχωρέω. Have students locate examples in the readings.

Grammar 3

Notes:

Exercise 6h

1. πρὸς τὸν ἀγρόν. . . .
   We are going to the field.
2. πρὸς τῇ ὁδῷ. . . .
   They are sitting by the road.
3. ἐκ τῆς οἰκίᾱς. . . .
   He hurries out of the house.
4. ἀπὸ τῆς νήσου. . . .
   They are sailing from the island.
5. κατὰ τὴν ὁδόν. . . .
   They are going down the road.
6. μετὰ τῶν ἑταίρων. . . .
   He flees with his comrades.
7. ἐν τῷ λαβυρίνθῳ. . . .
   Stay in the labyrinth. (*or* You are staying. . . .)
8. . . . πρὸς τὴν κρήνην.
   Lead us to the spring. (*or* You are leading us. . . .)
9. . . . ἀνὰ τὴν ὁδόν.
   The children are running up the road.
10. . . . ὑπὸ τῷ δένδρῳ.
    The girls are sitting under the tree.
11. . . . ἐπὶ τὸν λύκον.
    The dog rushes at the wolf.
12. . . . εἰς τὸν λαβύρινθον. . . .
    The comrades enter the labyrinth.

In no. 11, ὁρμᾶται is to be recalled from the second reading, where it is glossed. In no. 12, the compound verb εἰσέρχονται is to be deduced.

Exercise 6i

1. The man is not obeying you. (verb that is used with dative)
2. Obey me, boys. (verb that is used with dative)
3. Give me the plow. (indirect object)
4. I am telling the child the story. (I am telling the story to the child.) (indirect object)
5. The farmer has a plow. (possession)
6. The farmer, Dicaeopolis by name (called Dicaeopolis), leads the oxen into the field. (dative of respect, dative with verb)
7. The boy pelts the wolf with stones. (instrument)

8. The wife gives her husband much
    food. (. . . gives much food to her
    husband.) (indirect object)
9. The master calls the slaves with
    such a loud (great) shout that they
    are afraid. (means)
10. The boy has a beautiful dog.
    (possession)

In nos. 4 and 10, students can easily deduce the case of παιδί from the
definite article; likewise with βοῦσιν in
no. 6.
    Note the accent on ἔστι in nos. 5 and
10, when first in its clause.
    In no. 9, βοῇ is to be deduced (see
Word Building, Chapter 5).

Exercise 6j

1. ἆρ' οὐκ ἐθέλεις πείθεσθαί μοι, ὦ
    παῖ;
2. εἰπέ μοι τὸν μῦθον.
3. παρέχω σοι τὸ ἄροτρον.
4. ἔστι τῷ αὐτουργῷ μέγας βοῦς.
5. ὁ νεᾱνίᾱς, Θησεὺς ὀνόματι, τοῖς
    ἑταίροις ἀνδρείως ἡγεῖται.
6. ὁ παῖς τὸν λύκον λίθῳ τύπτει.
7. ἡ παρθένος/ἡ παῖς τὸν σῖτον τῇ
    φίλῃ/τῷ φίλῳ παρέχει.
8. ὁ δοῦλος τοὺς βοῦς τῷ κέντρῳ
    τύπτει.
9. ἡ παρθένος/ἡ παῖς ταῖς πύλαις
    προσχωρεῖ.
10. τῇ ὑστεραίᾳ οἱ Ἀθηναῖοι ἐκ-
    φεύγουσιν ἐκ τοῦ λαβυρίνθου.

Exercise 6k

1. Theseus wants to save his com-
    rades.
    ὁ Αἰγεὺς μάλα φοβεῖται ἀλλὰ
    πείθεται αὐτῷ.
2. The Athenians arrive at the island,
    and the king receives them.
    οἱ μὲν ἑταῖροι μάλα (μάλιστα)
    φοβοῦνται, ὁ δὲ Θησεὺς ἀνδρείως
    ἡγεῖται αὐτοῖς.
3. Don't fight, friends, and don't shout
    but be quiet.
    μὴ φοβεῖσθε τὸν Μῑνώταυρον, ὦ
    φίλοι, ἀλλ' ἀνδρεῖοι ἔστε.
4. When night falls, the girl goes to the
    gates.

ἐπεὶ γίγνεται ἡ ἡμέρᾱ, ἡ ναῦς εἰς
τὴν νῆσον ἀφικνεῖται.
5. When Theseus kills the Minotaur,
    we follow him out of the labyrinth.
    ἐπεὶ πρὸς τὴν Κρήτην πορευόμεθα,
    πολλὰς νήσους ὁρῶμεν.

Illustration (page 66)

Drawn from an Attic red figure cup
by the Foundry Painter, ca. 470 B.C.
(Tarquinia, Museo Nazionale). While
Eros hovers over the sleeping Ariadne,
Hermes is ready to lead Theseus away.

Ο ΘΗΣΕΥΣ
ΤΗΝ ΑΡΙΑΔΝΗΝ
ΚΑΤΑΛΕΙΠΕΙ

Title: "Theseus Deserts Ariadne"

Students have had λείπω meaning "I
leave" and κατά meaning "down."
Here the prepositional prefix merely in-
tensifies the meaning of the verb. Students will have no trouble with the title,
especially after looking at the illustration on page 66.

Translation

Lines 1–9
    So Theseus saves his comrades and
escapes from Crete. And so first they
sail to a certain island, called Naxos.
And when they arrive, they disembark
from the ship and rest. And when night
falls, the others sleep; but Theseus does
not sleep but stays quiet; for he does not
love Ariadne and does not want to take
her to Athens. And so soon, when Ariadne is asleep, Theseus wakes his comrades and says, "Be quiet, friends; it is
time to sail away. And so hurry to the
ship." And so when they arrive at the
ship, they quickly loosen the cables and
sail away; and Ariadne they leave on
the island.

[Word glossed earlier in chapter:
ὀνόματι by name.]

Lines 10–13

But when day comes, Ariadne wakes up and sees that neither Theseus nor his comrades are there. And so she runs to the shore and looks toward the sea; but she does not see the ship. And so she is very afraid and shouts, "Theseus, where are you? Are you deserting me? Come back and save me."

Exercise 6l

1.   ἐν ᾧ καλεῖ ἡ Ἀριάδνη, ὁ θεὸς Διόνῦσος ἀπὸ τοῦ οὐρανοῦ βλέπει πρὸς τὴν γῆν· ὁρᾷ οὖν τὴν Ἀρι-άδνην καὶ φιλεῖ αὐτήν (ἐρᾷ αὐτῆς).

2.   πέτεται οὖν ἀπὸ τοῦ οὐρανοῦ πρὸς τὴν γῆν. ἐπεὶ δὲ ἀφικνεῖται εἰς τὴν νῆσον, προσχωρεῖ αὐτῇ καί, "ὦ Ἀριάδνη," φησίν, "μὴ φοβοῦ· ἐγὼ γὰρ πάρειμι, Διόνῦσος. φιλῶ σε (ἐρῶ σου) καὶ βούλομαι σῴζειν. ἐλθὲ μετά μου πρὸς τὸν οὐρανόν."

3.   ἡ οὖν Ἀριάδνη χαίρει καὶ ἔρχεται πρὸς αὐτόν.

4.   ὁ οὖν Διόνῦσος ἀναφέρει αὐτὴν πρὸς τὸν οὐρανόν· ἡ δὲ Ἀριάδνη θεὰ γίγνεται καὶ μένει ἐν τῷ οὐρανῷ εἰσαιεί.

7
Ο ΚΥΚΛΩΨ (α)

Title: "The Cyclops"

The purposes of this chapter are:

1. Reading: to continue and conclude the mythological digression by having Philip tell the story of Odysseus and the Cyclops and by rounding out the story of Theseus and Ariadne with the story of the death of Theseus' father upon Theseus' return to Athens
2. Grammar: (a) to introduce the concept of declensions of nouns and to present the declension of typical third declension nouns with consonant stems; (b) to present the forms of the reflexive pronouns; and (c) to present another third declension consonant stem noun and the forms and use of the third declension interrogative/indefinite pronoun/adjective
3. Background: to present a discussion of Homer, the *Iliad*, and the *Odyssey*, to accompany the story of Odysseus and the Cyclops

Illustration

Drawn from an Attic black figure oinochoe by the Theseus Painter, ca. 500 B.C. (Paris, Louvre).

Caption under Illustration

"Odysseus drives the stake into the one eye of the Cyclops": the proper names at the beginning and end will be readily recognizable, especially since the nominative ὁ Κύκλωψ stands as the title of the chapter. Students will be happy to recognize ἐλαύνει and will then easily deduce τὸ ῥόπαλον and τὸν ἕνα ὀφθαλμόν from the illustration.

The caption includes three third declension words, two of which (ἕνα and

Κύκλωπος) have endings that will be presented in this chapter.

Vocabulary

The aorist infinitive εἰπεῖν was glossed in readings 5β and 6β; we include it in this vocabulary list to be learned, along with the imperatives εἰπέ and εἴπετε.

Note that we also include the infinitive ἰέναι in this list. The imperatives ἴθι and ἴτε "go" were given in Vocabulary 5α. These are respectively the infinitive and imperative of εἶμι (stem ἰ-/εἰ-; compare Latin ī-re). The verb is irregular and will not be given in full until Chapter 17.

The word θάλαττα appears here because it is first used in a main reading in this chapter (7α:18); students will be familiar with it from the grammar section on first declension nouns in Chapter 4 and from the reading at the end of Chapter 6.

For presentation and paradigms of the reflexive pronouns, see Grammar 3.

Translation

Lines 1–6
But when Myrrhine finishes her story, Melissa says, "How beautiful the story is! Tell us some other story, mother." But Myrrhine says, "No, for now I intend to prepare dinner." And so Melissa cries, but Philip says, "Don't cry, Melissa; for I am willing to tell you a story about a much-traveled man, called Odysseus.

Lines 7–12
"For Odysseus sails to Troy with Agamemnon and the Achaeans. And so for ten years they fight around Troy, and finally they take the city. And so Odysseus tells (orders) his comrades to go on board the ships, and they sail away homeward from Troy. But on the way they suffer many terrible things. For often they undergo storms, and often they fall into other very great dangers.

[Note that in the phrase ἐν ... τῇ ὁδῷ (10–11) "on" is a better translation than "in."

Note that in πολλὰ καὶ δεινά (11) Greek regularly joins two (or more) adjectives by καί or τε ... καί, while English does not usually use connectives between two adjectives.]

Lines 13–17

"Once they sail to a certain little island, and get out of the ships and make dinner on the shore. There is another island near; they see smoke and hear the sound of sheep and goats. And so the next day Odysseus tells his comrades to go on board the ship; for he wants to sail to the island and learn who lives there.

[Students should be clearly informed that the preposition εἰς may be used with verbs of motion and nouns indicating destinations with the meaning "to," and not "into," e.g., πλέουσί ... εἰς νῆσόν τινα μικράν "They sail ... to a certain small island" (13).

Note the accent on ἔστι (14); the word is so accented when it stands at the beginning of a clause; when so used it means "there is."

οἰῶν (15): the word is glossed here and its subsequent uses are accompanied by articles that will indicate case. The full declension need not be presented to students, but we give it here for the teacher: οἶς, οἰός, οἰί, οἶν; οἶες, οἰῶν, οἰσί, οἶς.

Note that the clause τίνες ἐκεῖ οἰκοῦσιν "what men live there" (17) is plural, where English idiom would use the singular "who lives there," even if it refers to more than one person.]

Lines 18–26

"And so soon they arrive at the island. Near the sea they see a large cave and many sheep and many goats. And so Odysseus says to his comrades, 'You stay by the ship, but I intend to go into the cave.' And so he orders twelve of his companions to follow him, and the others stay by the ship. But when they arrive at the cave, they find no man inside. And so his comrades say, 'Odysseus, there is no man inside. And so drive the sheep and the goats to the ship and sail away as quickly as possible.'

[Compound verb to be deduced: εἰσιέναι (21).]

Lines 27–29

"But Odysseus refuses (is unwilling) to do this; for he wants to learn (find out) who lives in the cave. His comrades are very afraid, but nevertheless they obey Odysseus and remain in the cave."

Word Study

1. *Myth*: students will recognize the relationship between the English word *myth* and the root of ὁ μῦθος, but they have been given only one meaning of the Greek word, namely "story." This will put them on the right track, but you may want to say something of the range of meanings the Greek word had: (1) a word, speech, saying, (2) a story, narrative, and (3) fiction, as opposed to history. English has limited the word to the last meaning, fiction concerned especially with supernatural beings.

2. *mythology*: ἡ μῡθολογίᾱ = ὁ μῦθος + -λογίᾱ.

3. *polytheist*: students will recognize the roots of πολύς, πολλή, πολύ "much," (plural) "many" and of θεός. The Greek word πολύθεος, -ον meant "belonging to many gods" or "believing in many gods."

4. *pantheist*: πᾶς, παντ-ός + ὁ θεός + -ist = one who believes that God is everything.

5. *monotheist*: students will be slightly misled here, since as a combining form in English *mono-* means "one," while the Greek word μόνος means not "one" but "alone," "only." A *monotheist* is a person who believes in *one* god. The word *monotheist* is a post-classical formation; μόνος + θεός does not

appear as a compound in ancient Greek.

6. *atheist*: ἀ-privative + ὁ θεός + -ist = one who denies the existence of God (compare ἄθεος, -ον "denying the gods").

7. *theology*: ἡ θεολογίᾱ = ὁ θεός + -λογίᾱ = "the study of things divine."

Grammar 1

Notes:

Grammar 2

Note the accents on the ultima in the genitive and dative singular and dative plural of παῖς, regular with third declension nouns with monosyllabic stems. Normally such nouns circumflex the ultima of the genitive plural (e.g., θηρῶν from θήρ, "wild beast"); παίδων is an exception.

Exercise 7a

1. ἀνδρός (6): gen. sing., with preposition περί
2. ὀνόματι (6): dat. sing., dative of respect
3. Ἀγαμέμνονος (7): gen. sing., with preposition μετά
4. χειμῶνας (11): acc. pl., object of ὑπέχουσι
5. οἰῶν (15): gen. pl., possessive genitive with φθογγήν
6. αἰγῶν (15): gen. pl., possessive genitive with φθογγήν
7. αἶγας (19): acc. pl., object of ὁρῶσι

Exercise 7b

1. τῷ 2. τοῖς 3. τὸν 4. τῷ 5. τὰ 6. αἱ 7. ταῖς 8. τὰς 9. τῶν 10. τῇ 11. τὴν 12. τῷ 13. τὸν 14. τοὺς 15. οἱ 16. ταῖς 17. τῷ 18. τὸν/τὴν 19. ταῖς 20. τοῖς/ταῖς

Grammar 3

Notes:

Exercise 7c

1. The boy gets up (lifts himself) and hurries to the field.
2. ἑαυτούς. The boys get themselves up and hurry to the field.
3. Get up, wife (woman), and come here!
4. ὑμᾶς αὐτάς. Get up, women, and come here!
5. I don't wish (I refuse) to get up; for I am very tired.
6. ἡμᾶς αὐτάς. We don't wish (we refuse) to get up; for we are very tired.
7. To whom is the girl telling the story? Is she telling (it) to herself?
8. The father makes his daughter sit down with him.
9. ἑαυτοῖς. The fathers make their daughters sit down with them.
10. The boy sees his father's dog but does not see his own.
11. Don't go into the cave, friends; for you are leading yourselves into very great danger.
12. Help us, Odysseus; for we cannot save ourselves.

The verb καθίζει has so far been met only in its intransitive sense (e.g., ὁ Δικαιόπολις καθίζει ὑπὸ τῷ δένδρῳ), but it may also be used transitively (in a causative sense), as here (nos. 8 and 9).

Homer

Illustration (page 74)

This bust of Homer is a Roman copy of a Greek original, ca 150 B.C. (London, British Museum). Homer, according to tradition, was blind and lived on the island of Chios. See the Homeric *Hymn to Apollo* 167–172: "When any stranger comes here and asks, 'Who is the sweetest of the poets that come here and whom do you most enjoy?' remember me and all of you answer, 'He is a blind man and lives on rugged Chios.'"

Illustration (page 75)

From an Attic red figure neck amphora by the Kleophrades Painter, ca. 500 B.C. (London, British Museum). Rhapsodes were reciters of epic poetry; originally the term could apply to poets reciting their own poetry or to minstrels performing the works of others. Later, rhapsodes became a class of professional reciters, principally of Homer. They carried a staff, as in this painting.

For further reading, see *The World of Athens*, pp. 128–130, and *The Oxford History of the Classical World*, Chapter 2, "Homer," pp. 50–77.

Ο ΚΥΚΛΩΨ (β)

Illustration

Based on a detail from an Attic black figure crater by the Sappho Painter, ca. 510 B.C. (Badisches Museum, Karlsruhe).

Caption under Illustration

"Odysseus escapes from the cave of the Cyclops": ἄντρον was glossed in passage α:19.

Vocabulary

We introduce the periphrastic future (μέλλω + infinitive), which Attic authors used with the present or future infinitive to express intention: "I am about to, am (destined) to, intend to." Students should be strictly warned not to confuse this with the future indicative, which will occasionally be used (and glossed) in the readings before it is formally introduced in Chapter 17.

From this point on in the course we will begin to note the meanings of verbs when used in the middle voice (usually intransitive); students should be alert to the fact that many verbs will appear in both active and middle forms, often with different meanings or functions (e.g., transitive in the active and intransitive in the middle).

Latin students will be pleased to recognize the similarity of ϝοῖνος to *vīnum*.

Encourage students to see the relationship between εἷς, μία, ἕν and οὐδείς, οὐδεμία, οὐδέν in Vocabulary α.

Paradigms of εἷς and πᾶς will be given in Chapter 8, Grammar 4 and Grammar 5. The forms students will encounter in the present chapter are given in the vocabulary entry.

The adjective σώφρων is included in the vocabulary list although it does not occur in the story; it is used in the grammar section as an example of a third declension adjective and will be used in exercises.

Encourage students to see the relationship between ἐνθάδε and οἴκαδε (vocabulary 4β).

Translation

Lines 1–8

"Soon they hear a very great noise and in comes a fearful giant; for he is a monster; there is one eye in the middle of his forehead. And so Odysseus and his comrades are very afraid and flee to the corner of the cave. But the giant first drives his flocks into the cave, and when they are all inside, he lifts a huge (very big) stone and puts it in (into) the entrance of the cave. Then first he milks his flocks, and then he lights a fire. So he sees Odysseus and his comrades and, 'Strangers,' he shouts, 'Who are you and where are you sailing from?'

[Compound verb to be deduced: ἔνεστιν (3).]

Lines 9–10

"And Odysseus says, 'We are Achaeans and we are sailing home from Troy. A storm drives us here.'

Lines 11–13

"The Cyclops answers nothing but rushes at the Achaeans; and two of the comrades he seizes and bashes onto the ground; and their brains run out and wet the ground."

Lines 14–16

But Melissa says, "Stop, Philip, stop; for it's a terrible story (the story is terrible). But tell me, how does Odysseus escape? Does the Cyclops kill all his comrades?"

[It may be observed that Greek frequently uses the active form παῦε in an intransitive sense (simply "stop!").]

Lines 17–23

And Philip says, "No, the Cyclops does not kill (them) all. For Odysseus is a cunning man. And so first he gives the Cyclops lots of (much) wine, so that soon he is very drunk. And when the Cyclops is sleeping, Odysseus finds a huge stake and tells (orders) his comrades to heat it in the fire. And when the stake is about to catch fire, Odysseus lifts it from the fire and drives it into the one eye of the Cyclops.

Lines 24–26

"And he leaps up and shrieks terribly. And Odysseus and his comrades flee to the far corner of the cave. But the Cyclops cannot see them; for he is blind."

Lines 27–28

And Melissa says, "How clever Odysseus is! But how do they escape from the cave?"

Lines 29–33

And Philip says, "The next day as soon as (when first) the sun rises, the Cyclops lifts the stone from the entrance of the cave and sends out all his flocks. And so Odysseus hides his comrades under the sheep. So the Cyclops sends out the Achaeans with the sheep, and they drive the sheep to the ship and sail away."

[Compound verb to be deduced: ἐκπέμπει.]

Word Building

The pairs illustrate the formation of denominative verbs from nouns by adding to the noun stem the suffix -αζω/-αζομαι.

1. preparation; I prepare
2. name; I name
3. marvel; I wonder at, am amazed, admire
4. work; I work

Grammar 4

For the dative plural of consonant stem nouns, see Reference Grammar, pages 214–215.

Grammar 5

Notes:

Grammar 6

Notes:

Grammar 7

Notes:

Exercise 7d

1. αἱ γυναῖκες τῑμῶσι τὰς σώφρονας παρθένους.
   The women honor the well-behaved girls.
2. οἱ ἄνδρες μύθους τινὰς ταῖς παισὶ λέγουσιν.
   The men are telling some stories to the (female) children.
3. μὴ φοβεῖσθε τοὺς χειμῶνας, ὦ φίλοι.
   Don't fear the storms, friends.
4. βουλόμεθα γιγνώσκειν τίνες ἐν τοῖς ἄντροις οἰκοῦσιν.
   We want to know who (what men) live(s) in the caves.
5. οἱ παῖδες οὐ βούλονται ἡγεῖσθαι ἡμῖν πρὸς τὰς θαλάττᾱς.
   The boys do not want to lead us to the seas.

Exercise 7e

1. ἀγνοῶ τὸ τοῦ παιδὸς ὄνομα.
   I do not know the child's name.
2. ὁ πατὴρ τὸν παῖδα κελεύει τῑμᾶν τὸν θεόν.

Father orders the boy to honor the
god.

3. εἰπέ μοι τί ποιεῖ ὁ ἀνήρ.
   Tell me what the man is doing.

4. παῖς τις τὸν κύνα εἰς τὸν ἀγρὸν
   εἰσάγει.
   A boy is leading the dog into the
   field.

5. ἡ μήτηρ οὐκ ἐθέλει τῇ θυγατρὶ πρὸς
   τὴν πόλιν ἡγεῖσθαι.
   The mother is not willing (refuses)
   to lead her daughter to the city.

Exercise 7f

1. Who lives in the cave? A certain
   terrifying giant lives in the cave.
2. Whom do you see in the house? I see
   a certain woman in the house.
3. Whom are you leading to the city? I
   am leading some slaves to the city.
4. Whose plow are you carrying to the
   field? I am carrying the plow of a
   certain friend.
5. Whose is this dog (to whom is this
   dog)? It belongs (is) to my father.

Ο ΤΟΥ ΘΗΣΕΩΣ ΠΑΤΗΡ
ΑΠΟΘΝΗΙΣΚΕΙ

Title: "Theseus' Father Dies"

You will need to give students the
meaning of the verb.

Translation

Lines 1–8

When Theseus is about to sail away
to Crete, his father says to him, "I am
very afraid for you, my son; but nevertheless go to Crete and both kill the
Minotaur and save your comrades; then
hurry home. While you are away, I will
go up onto the top of the promontory every
day, wishing to see your ship. But listen
to me; the ship has sails (that are) black.
If you kill the Minotaur and save your
comrades, hurry home, and when you
approach Athens, take down the black
sails and raise sails (that are) white.
For so I will learn that you are safe."

[This paragraph has two verbs in the future tense (ἀναβήσομαι, 4, and γνώσομαι,
8) and four subjunctives (ἄπῃς, 4,
ἀποκτείνῃς, 6, σώσῃς, 6, and προσχωρῇς,
7). The glosses will suffice, and no discussion of the forms is needed.

Note the use of adjectives in the
predicate position: τὰ ἱστία μέλανα, 5,
and τὰ ἱστία λεῦκα, 7. We suggest
translating the adjectives as relative
clauses (see above).]

Lines 9–11

And so Theseus says that he intends
to obey his father and sails away to
Crete. And Aegeus goes every day up
onto the top of the promontory and looks
out to sea.

Lines 12–17

But when Theseus leaves Ariadne
on Naxos and is hurrying home, he for-
gets his father's words, and he does not
take down the black sails. And so
Aegeus recognizes the ship, but he sees
that it has black sails. And so he is very
afraid for Theseus. He shouts loudly
and throws himself from the cliff into
the sea and so dies. For this reason the
sea is called (the) Aegean Sea/the name
for the sea is (the) Aegean Sea.

Exercise 7g

1. ἐπεὶ ὁ Θησεὺς εἰς τὰς Ἀθήνᾱς
   ἀφικνεῖται, γιγνώσκει ὅτι τέθνηκεν ὁ
   πατήρ.
2. ἡ μήτηρ τῷ νεᾱνίᾳ, "σύ," φησίν,
   "αἴτιος εἶ· αἰεὶ γὰρ τῶν τοῦ πατρὸς
   λόγων λανθάνῃ.
3. ὁ Θησεὺς μάλα λῡπεῖται καί, "ἐγώ,"
   φησίν, "αἴτιός εἰμι. ἐν νῷ οὖν ἔχω
   ἀπὸ τοῦ οἴκου ἀποφεύγειν.
4. ἡ δὲ μήτηρ κελεύει αὐτὸν μὴ
   ἀπιέναι.
5. δι' ὀλίγου βασιλεὺς γίγνεται, καὶ
   πάντες οἱ Ἀθηναῖοι φιλοῦσιν αὐτὸν
   καὶ τῑμῶσιν.

In no. 5, note that the word order is
the same in "all the Athenians" and in
πάντες οἱ Ἀθηναῖοι.

8
ΠΡΟΣ ΤΟ ΑΣΤΥ (α)

Title: "To the City"

Students will already be familiar with the phrase used as the title of this chapter; see passage 4α·21.

The purposes of this chapter are:

1. Reading: to resume the narrative of the main story line from where we left off at the end of Chapter 5 (passage 8α picks up the two themes of the slaying of the wolf by Philip and his dog and of the arrival of the messenger reporting the imminent festival in Athens; passage β records the family's trip to Athens); to continue the sequence of stories from the *Odyssey* begun in Chapter 7, with the story of Aeolus at the end of this chapter (the sequence continues through the readings at the ends of the next two chapters)

2. Grammar: (α) to introduce the forms of the present middle participle and the middle voice of -α- contract verbs; (β) to introduce the forms of more third declension nouns and of πᾶς and to introduce the cardinal and ordinal numbers from "one" to "ten" and the declension of the ordinals from "first" to "tenth"

3. Background: to present a survey of Athenian history from the Bronze Age to the Age of Pericles

Illustration

Drawn from a lekythos by the Amasis Painter, ca. 560 B.C. (New York, Metropolitan Museum). Another scene from this vase appears in the illustration on page 41.

Caption under Illustration

"The women, talking to one another, weave cloth": students should deduce the meaning of the verb ὑφαίνουσιν from the actions of the women in the picture. They will get διαλεγόμεναι from the first entry in the vocabulary list. For the meanings of πέπλον and ἀλλήλαις, it may be easiest to refer students to the glosses under the first paragraph of the reading.

Try to get students to deduce the meaning of the *form* of the participle διαλεγόμεναι and have them try different translations to find one that best fits the context, e.g.: "conversing," "while conversing," "who are conversing." The participle is one of the main new features of grammar in this chapter, and if students learn to recognize it from the characteristic letters -μεν- here it will help them with the reading.

Vocabulary

For a discussion of the difference between ἄστυ and πόλις, see the teacher's notes to Chapter 10, Grammar 1 (p. 57).

Translation

Lines 1–17

Meanwhile Dicaeopolis and the slave are working in the field. When evening comes, they loosen the oxen and drive (them) home. At home Myrrhine and her daughter are weaving cloth; and while they weave, they converse with one another. Soon the mother sees her husband coming into the courtyard. And so she stops working and hurries to the door and says, "Greetings, husband; come here and listen. For Philip and Argus have killed a wolf." And he said, "Are you telling the truth? Tell me what happened." And so Myrrhine relates everything, and he is amazed and says, "Well done; the boy is brave and strong. But tell me, where is he? For I want to honor the wolf-slayer." And he intends to look for the boy. But Myrrhine says, "But wait, dear, and listen again. For a messenger has come from the city; and he says that the Athenians are celebrating (making for themselves) the festival of (for) Dionysus. Won't you (are you not willing to) take me and the children to the festival?" But he says, "But it's not possible, wife; for it is necessary to work. For hunger follows the lazy man, as the poet says; but from work(s) men become rich in flocks and wealthy."

[Having seen the form and use of the participle διαλεγόμεναι in the caption under the illustration, students should be ready to recognize and understand the use of the participles εἰσερχόμενον (5) and ἐργαζομένη (5) in this paragraph.

Students have seen παύω used intransitively in the form of the imperative παῦε (reading 7β:14). In lines 5 and 20–21 of the present reading, the verb is used in the middle voice with a supplementary participle; students should have no trouble with the translation, e.g., παύεται ἐργαζομένη "she stops working."

Students may note that we now use the middle voice in the phrase τὴν ἑορτὴν ποιοῦνται (13), while in the readings in Chapter 4 we used the active voice (ἑορτὴν ποιοῦσιν). Both voices are used in the Greek authors, and since students have now had the middle voice, we use it here.

At the end of the paragraph Dicaeopolis quotes from Hesiod's *Works and Days* 302 (λῑμὸς γάρ τοι πάμπαν ἀεργῷ σύμφορος ἀνδρί, "for hunger is always a companion of the lazy man"), which he paraphrases, and 308 (ἐξ ἔργων δ' ἄνδρες πολύμηλοί τ' ἀφνειοί τε, "from work men become rich in flocks and wealthy"), which he quotes precisely. Hesiod's poem (8th –7th centuries B.C.) is largely concerned with farming and might well have been Dicaeopolis's favorite reading.]

Lines 18–21

But Myrrhine says, "But nevertheless take us there, dear husband. For we rarely journey to the city; everyone is going." But he says, "But (it's) impossible; for the slave is lazy; for whenever I'm away, he stops working.

Lines 22–27

But Melissa says, "But don't be hard, father, but obey us. Don't you also wish to see the festival and honor the god? For Dionysus saves our vines (the vines for us). And Philip—don't you want to honor the boy because he has killed the wolf? For he wants to see the competitions and the dances. And so take us all to the city."

[τὴν ἑορτὴν θεᾶσθαι (23): in 4α:22 we used the verb θεωρέω in a similar context; both verbs may be used of seeing festivals and games (see the opening of Plato's *Republic*).]

Lines 28–29

And Dicaeopolis says, "Very well! since that's what you want. But I tell you that hunger is destined to follow us—but *I* am not to blame."

Word Study

1. *politics:* from τὰ πολῑτικά, the adjective made from ἡ πόλις. Politics is thus the affairs of the citizens or of the city.
2. *politburo:* πολῑτ- + buro (= French *bureau*); a hybrid formation (U.S.S.R.) = "the office of state," "the government."
3. *metropolis:* from the Greek word ἡ μητρόπολις = "mother city" (especially of the relationship between a founding city and a colony, also of one's homeland and of a capital city or chief town).
4. *necropolis;* ἡ νεκρόπολις = "city of the dead," the name given to a suburb of Alexandria.
5. *cosmopolitan:* ὁ κοσμοπολίτης = "a citizen of the world" rather than of a particular city (attested in ancient literature).

Grammar 1

Notes:

Exercise 8a

1. The women stop working.
   (ἐργαζόμεναι: feminine nominative
   plural agreeing with αἱ γυναῖκες)
2. Philip sees his father coming into
   the house. (εἰσερχόμενον: masculine
   accusative singular agreeing with
   τὸν πατέρα)
3. Wishing to see the festival, we are
   hurrying to the city. (βουλόμενοι:
   masculine nominative plural
   agreeing with "we"—subject of
   σπεύδομεν)
4. Do you see the boys following the
   beautiful girls? (ἑπομένους: masculine accusative plural agreeing with
   τοὺς παῖδας)
5. The girls, being very afraid, run
   home as quickly as possible.
   (φοβούμεναι: feminine nominative
   plural agreeing with αἱ παρθένοι)
6. Do you hear the women talking with
   one another in the house?
   (διαλεγομένων feminine genitive
   plural agreeing with τῶν γυναικῶν)

Exercise 8b

1. ἆρ' ὁρᾷς τοὺς παῖδας ἐν τῇ ὁδῷ
   μαχομένους;
2. ὁ Δικαιόπολις παύεται ἐργαζόμενος
   καὶ τοὺς βοῦς οἴκαδε ἐλαύνει.
3. παῦε μοι ἑπόμενος καὶ ἄπελθε.
4. τῷ πατρὶ πειθομένη ἡ παρθένος
   οἴκοι μένει.
5. τοῖς ἑταίροις ἀνδρείως ἡγούμενος ὁ
   Θησεὺς ἐκ τοῦ λαβυρίνθου ἐκφεύγει.
6. οἱ ἄνθρωποι/ἄνδρες πολλὰ καὶ δεινὰ
   πάσχουσι πρὸς/εἰς τὴν νῆσον
   πορευόμενοι.

In no. 3, note that the active imperative form παῦε is regularly used intransitively.
In no. 6, students should be warned
that "things" is not to be translated with
a separate word but is implied in the
neuter plural adjectives, which are used
as substantives.

Grammar 2

Notes:

Exercise 8c

Sets of forms of this sort are not provided
in this handbook; teachers should check
students' work carefully.

Athens:
A Historical Outline

Illustration (page 88)

Relief from Persepolis, Council
Hall, showing figures of Persian guards
on stairway balustrade; Achaemenid
Period, fifth century B.C.; excavated and
photographed by the Persepolis Expedition of The Oriental Institute of the University of Chicago. (Teheran, Archaeological Museum).

Illustration (page 89)

Bust of Pericles, Roman copy of
Greek original, ca. 440 B.C. (London,
British Museum).

For further reading, see *The World
of Athens*, pp. 1–24, and *The Oxford History of the Classical World*, pp. 26–35.

ΠΡΟΣ ΤΟ ΑΣΤΥ (β)

Illustration

Drawn from a cup by the Niobid
Painter, ca. 450 B.C. (London, British
Museum).

Caption under Illustration

"Dicaeopolis, making a libation,
prays to Zeus to keep all safe": encourage students to deduce σπονδήν; they will
find τὸν Δία and the verb εὔχομαι in the
vocabulary list.
Students may find the word order
and the two accusatives troublesome: "he

prays (to) Zeus to keep all safe" or "he prays (that) Zeus keep all safe."

Vocabulary

Notes:

Translation

Lines 1–11

And so on the next day as soon as day comes, Myrrhine wakes up and wakes her husband and says, "Get yourself up, husband; it is not possible to sleep any longer; it is time to journey to the city." And so her husband gets up; and first he calls Xanthias and tells him not to be lazy and not to stop working. Meanwhile Myrrhine brings food and wakes grandfather and the children. Then Dicaeopolis goes into the courtyard and leads the others to the altar; and making a libation he prays to Zeus to (prays that Zeus) keep all safe as they go to the city. Finally he leads out the mule, and grandfather gets up onto it. And so they journey to the city.

[Word glossed earlier in chapter: ἀργός lazy (5).

σπονδὴν . . . ποιούμενος (8–9): note the middle voice.

Compound verbs to be deduced (10): ἐξάγει and ἀναβαίνει. The verb ἀνα-βαίνω with ἐπί and the accusative was used in the reading at the end of Chapter 7 in the sense "to go up onto" (the top of the promontory. Here it means "to get up onto" (the mule).]

Lines 12–17

The road is long and difficult. Soon Myrrhine is tired and wants to sit down; and the mule is tired too and refuses to go on (forward). And so they sit by the road and rest. But soon Dicaeopolis says, "It is time to go on; cheer up, wife; the road is long and difficult at first, but when(ever) one gets to the top, as the poet says, then it becomes easy."

[μακρὰ γὰρ ἡ ὁδός (16): note omission of the verb.

In the last sentence we have kept the present general temporal clause with the subjunctive (as it is in Hesiod); it is translated in the gloss, and the grammar need not be discussed at this time. Dicaeopolis is paraphrasing Hesiod again, *Works and Days*, II. 290–292: μακρὸς δὲ καὶ ὄρθιος οἶμος ἐς αὐτὴν (i.e., τὴν ἀρετήν) / καὶ τρηχὺς τὸ πρῶτον· ἐπὴν δ᾽ εἰς ἄκρον ἵκηαι, / ῥηιδίη δὴ ἔπειτα πέλει, χαλεπή περ ἐοῦσα. "The road to it (i.e., virtue), is long and steep, and rough at first, but when you reach the top, she (i.e., virtue) then becomes easy indeed, although being difficult." Note that in Hesiod it is virtue that becomes easy when one reaches the top, whereas Dicaeopolis simplifies the moral by saying that the road then becomes easy.]

Lines 18–23

And so they go on up the hill, and when they arrive at the top they see Athens lying below. And Philip gazing at the city, says, "Look! How beautiful the city is! Do you see the Acropolis?" And Melissa says, "I do see it. Do you see the Parthenon too? How beautiful it is and big!" And Philip says, "But hurry, papa; we are going down toward the city."

[κάτω κειμένας (19): note the predicate position of the participle.

ὡς καλή (20): note ὡς used with an adjective in an exclamation.]

Lines 24–31

And so they quickly go down, and arriving at the gates they tie the mule to a tree and go in. In the city they see many people walking in the streets. For men and women, youths and children, citizens and foreigners, are hurrying to the agora (city center). And so Myrrhine fearing for her children says, "Come here, Philip, and take hold of my hand. And you—Melissa I mean—don't leave me but follow with me; for there are so many people that I am afraid for you."

[ἀφικόμενοι (24): sense requires the aorist.

ἄνδρες γὰρ γυναῖκες νεᾶνίαι παῖδες (26–27): note the asyndeton (absence of connectives).

πολῖται τε καὶ ξένοι (27): apposition.]

Word Building

1. where? where to? from where?
2. there; to there; from there
3. at home; to home; from home
4. in another place; to another place; from another place
5. everywhere; in all directions; from all directions
6. in Athens; to Athens; from Athens

For place where, the suffixes are -ου, -ι, -θι, and -σι(ν); for place to which, they are -σε, -δε, and -ζε (ποῖ is an exception, but it is the form used in Attic Greek; πόσε, the regular form, is confined to Homer and epic); and for place from which, -θεν.

Grammar 3

Notes:

Grammar 4

Notes:

Grammar 5

Students should learn the numbers 1–3 carefully, including the full paradigms. They should become familiar enough with the numbers 4–10 (cardinals and ordinals) to be able to recognize them with ease in the readings. These numbers will not be given in the chapter vocabularies or glossed in subsequent readings, but they are all included in the vocabularies at the end of the book for reference.

Remind students that οὐδείς is a compound of the negative οὐδέ + εἷς.

Students should be told that the δυοῖν (genitive and dative) have endings regularly used in the dual number for second declension nouns and adjectives. Homer has δύω, which also shows the original dual ending.

Exercise 8d

1. The farmer has two sons and one daughter.
2. The mother gives the daughter no food.
3. On the third day the daughter tells her father everything.
4. The father calls the mother and the boys.
5. He says to the mother, "You have three children. Why do you give food to two and nothing to one?"
6. "You must give food to all (of them)."
7. And the woman obeys her husband and gives food to all the children.
8. The daughters, obeying their mother, wake their father and persuade him to go to Athens.
9. The father leaves his sons at home and leads his daughters to Athens.
10. The road is long and difficult, but on the second day they arrive there.
11. They see many people in the roads rushing in all directions.
12. When they arrive at the agora, they stay a long time looking at everything.
13. For two days they look at the things in the agora, and on the third they go up onto the Acropolis.
14. They stay in Athens for nine days, and on the tenth they start home.
15. They journey for four days, traveling slowly, and on the fifth they arrive home.

Sentences 8, 9, 10, 11, 14, and 15 provide practice with words indicating place that were presented in the Word Building exercise on page 92.

In no. 11, students should recognize σπεύδοντας as the same form as βαδίζοντας, which they met in passage β:26.

In sentences 12–15 attention can be called to the distinction between the accusative of extent of time and the dative of time when.

Students may need help with the substantive use of the article in the phrase τὰ ἐν τῇ ἀγορᾷ "the things in the agora" in no. 13.

Note the middle voice ποιοῦνται in no. 15.

ΟΔΥΣΣΕΥΣ ΚΑΙ Ο ΑΙΟΛΟΣ

Title: "Odysseus and Aeolus"

Based on *Odyssey* 10.1–75.

Translation

Lines 1–3

When we escape from the cave of the Cyclops, we return quickly to our comrades. And when they see us, they rejoice. The next day I tell them to go onto the ship again. So we sail away.

Lines 4–7

Soon we arrive at the island of Aeolia. There lives Aeolus, king of the winds. And he, receiving us kindly, entertains us for a long time. And when I tell him to send us away, he gives me a bag in(to) which he ties up all the winds except one, a gentle west wind.

Lines 8–11

And so for nine days we sail on, and on the tenth we see our fatherland. At that very moment I fall asleep; and my

comrades, when they see me sleeping, say this (speak thus): "What is in the bag? Surely there is much gold in it and much silver, gifts of Aeolus. Come on! Untie (loosen) the bag and take the gold."

Lines 12–16

But when they untie the bag, at once out fly all the winds, and they make a terrible storm and drive the ship away from our fatherland. And I wake up and learn what is happening. And so I despair and want to throw myself into the sea; but my comrades save me. So the winds carry us back again to the island of Aeolus.

[Compound verb to be deduced: ἀπελαύνουσιν (13).]

Exercise 8e

1. ἐπεὶ εἰς τὴν νῆσον ἀφικνούμεθα, πρὸς τὸν τοῦ Αἰόλου οἶκον ἔρχομαι.
2. ὁ δέ, ἐπεὶ ὁρᾷ με, μάλα θαυμάζει καί, "τί πάσχεις;" φησίν, "διὰ τί αὖθις πάρει;"
3. ἐγὼ δὲ ἀποκρίνομαι, "οἱ ἑταῖροι αἴτιοί εἰσιν· τοὺς γὰρ ἀνέμους ἔλῦσαν. ἀλλὰ βοήθει ἡμῖν, ὦ φίλε."
4. ὁ δὲ Αἴολος, "ἄπιθι ταχέως," φησίν, "ἀπὸ τῆς νήσου. οὐ γὰρ δυνατόν ἐστί σοι βοηθεῖν. οἱ γὰρ θεοὶ δήπου μῑσοῦσί σε."

In no. 4 students will have to cope with an enclitic (ἐστι) followed by another enclitic (σοι). See Reference Grammar, page 209.

9
Η ΠΑΝΗΓΥΡΙΣ (α)

Title: "The Festival"

Explain that the word πανήγυρις is a compound of πᾶς and ἡ ἄγυρις "gathering," and is used of a festival to which everyone comes to celebrate one of the major gods.

The purposes of this chapter are:

1. Reading: to record the experiences of the family on their arrival in Athens, to tour the Acropolis with them, and to describe the evening procession in honor of Dionysus and the prayers and rites in his honor (and in the story at the end of the chapter, to continue the series of tales from the *Odyssey* with the story of Odysseus and Circe)
2. Grammar: (α) to introduce the forms of the present active participle; (β) to present another third declension noun, to consolidate the uses of the genitive case, and to review some uses of the article
3. Background: to describe Athens as it might be experienced by an ancient visitor

Illustration (page 96 bottom)

The statue of Athena Parthenos, one of the masterworks of Pheidias, stood inside the east end of the cella of the Parthenon. Made of gold and ivory, it stood 38 feet or 11.5 meters high (including the base); the Victory in her right hand was 6 feet or 1.8 meters high. With her left hand she supports her spear and holds her shield, behind which curls a serpent, representing the spirit of Erechtheus, the mythical founder and king of Athens. The statue remained in the Parthenon until the fifth century A.D., when it was removed to Constantinople. It was still there in the tenth century but disappeared soon after (melted down?).

A model made ca. A.D. 120 survives, and this, together with a detailed description by Pausanias (fl. A.D. 150), makes possible the reconstruction shown in this photograph (Royal Ontario Museum, Canada).

Caption under Illustration

"They see the statue of Athena, being armed and carrying Victory in (her) right hand": there are a number of words here that students have not had, but their meanings can easily be elicited with content questions. "What do you see?" εἰκόνα "a statue." "How is the goddess clothed?" ἐνοπλίου "in armor." "What is she carrying?" Νίκην "Victory." "With what is she carrying it?" δεξιᾷ "with her right hand."

The caption introduces two present participles, οὔσης and φερούσης, and different translations may be tried, e.g., "being" and "which is" for οὔσης and "carrying" for φερούσης.

Vocabulary

Note that "to go up onto" or "to climb" is expressed with ἀναβαίνω + ἐπί "onto" + accusative. Students have seen this in the reading at the end of Chapter 7 (lines 4 and 10) and in 8β:10–11.

Note that ἐπανέρχομαι when it means "return to" will be used with εἰς or πρός "to" and the accusative.

Under the entry for ἐπί we have added "onto" as one of its meanings with the accusative (e.g., with ἀναβαίνω).

Translation

Lines 1–5
And so walking like this they arrive at the agora. But there is such a crowd there that they can scarcely go on toward the Acropolis. Finally, following Dicaeopolis, they arrive at a colonnade, and sitting down they watch the people hurrying and shouting and making a din.

[στοᾱ (3): students might wonder why
this word ends in an α that is not pre-
ceded by ε, ι, or ρ. Other spellings of the
word show the ι, e.g., στοιά.

σπεύδοντας, βοῶντας, and ποιοῦντας
(4–5): help students deduce the meanings of these participial forms. Two
present active participles occurred earlier (βαδίζοντας, 8β:26, and σπεύδοντας,
Exercise 8d, no. 11), the first of which
was glossed, so students should have
some familiarity with the form and the
meaning.]

Lines 6–11

By now the children are very hungry. And Philip sees a sausage-seller
pushing his way through the crowd and
hawking his wares. And so he calls his
father and says, "Dear papa, look! a
sausage-seller is coming this way.
Don't you want to buy some food? For we
are very hungry." And so Dicaeopolis
calls the sausage-seller and buys some
food. So they sit in the colonnade eating
sausages and drinking wine.

[The sausage-seller is a character from
one of the comedies of Aristophanes, the
Knights.

Students should deduce an appropriate meaning for βοῶντα (7), such as
"hawking."

Present active participles: βοῶντα
(7), ἐσθίοντες (11), and πίνοντες (11).]

Lines 12–16

After the meal Dicaeopolis says,
"Come on! Don't you want to climb the
Acropolis and look at the temples?"
Grandfather is very tired and refuses to
go up, and the others leave him sitting in
the colonnade, and pushing through the
crowd they go up onto the Acropolis.

Lines 17–22

And when they arrive at the top of the
Acropolis and pass through the gateway,
they see the temple of the Maiden opposite
and the statue of Athena, which is
(being) very large, fully armed and
carrying a spear in her right hand. And
so for a long time the children, gazing at

the goddess, remain quiet, but finally
Dicaeopolis says, "Come on! Don't you
want to look at the temple?" And he leads
them forward.

[Participles: οὖσαν and φέρουσαν (19);
the gloss will help with the former.]

Lines 23–33

The temple is huge and very beautiful. For a long time they look at the
carvings, which decorate the whole temple. The gates are open; and so the children go up and enter (the temple). The
whole inside is dark, but they just (with
difficulty) see opposite the statue of
Athena, the most beautiful work of Pheidias. The goddess gleams with gold,
carrying a (statue of) Victory in her
right hand, and in her left a shield. The
children, gazing, are both frightened
and rejoice. Philip goes forward, and
holding up his hands he prays to the goddess, "O Maiden Athena, daughter of
Zeus, protectress of our city, be gracious
and listen to my prayer (to me praying);
keep this city safe and keep us safe from
all dangers." Then he returns to
Melissa and leads her out of the temple.

[τὸ πᾶν ἱερόν (24): note the attributive
position of the adjective πᾶς when it
means "whole"; compare the predicate
position in the phrase οἱ παρόντες πάντες
in 9β:21. Mention may be made of the
different meanings of the adjective in its
different positions, which correspond to
a certain extent with English (τὸ πᾶν
ἱερόν "the whole temple," but πάντες οἱ
παρόντες "all those present."

πάντα τὰ εἴσω (25): note the use of
the article and adverb as a substantive,
"the things inside" = "the inside." Note
also the predicate position of the adjective
πάντα, literally, "all the things inside"
= "the whole inside."

Present active participle: φέρουσα
(28).

Note the use of the dative with εὔχεται
(30): "prays *to* the goddess."

Philip's prayer follows the traditional form: invocation of the god or

goddess with mention of his or her
birth—here "daughter of Zeus"—and a
cult title—here "protectress of our city";
this would usually be followed by a
promise of an offering such as a sacrifice; and finally there is the request
made to the deity.]

Lines 34–38

For a long time they look for their
parents, and finally they find them behind the temple looking down on the
sanctuary of Dionysus. And Dicaeopolis says, "Look, children! The people are
already gathering at the sanctuary. It's
time to go down and look for grandfather."

Lines 39–44

And so they go down and hurry to the
colonnade. There they find grandfather
in a bad temper: "What are you doing,
child?" he says; "Why do you leave me
so long? Why aren't we watching the
procession?" But Dicaeopolis says,
"Cheer up, papa. For we are now going to
the sanctuary of Dionysus; for the procession takes place soon. Come on!" So
he speaks and leads them to the sanctuary.

Word Study

1. *democracy*: ἡ δημοκρατίᾱ (ὁ δῆμος
   + τὸ κράτος = "power," "rule"). The
   English noun suffix -*cy* regularly
   replaces Greek noun endings -τίᾱ,
   -τείᾱ, -κίᾱ, and -κείᾱ).

2. *demagogue*: ὁ δημαγωγός (ὁ δῆμος +
   ἄγω, ἀγωγός, -όν = "leading"); "a
   leader of the people" (the word is now
   used in a pejorative sense of a politi-
   cian who unscrupulously appeals to
   the emotions and selfish interests of
   the electorate).

3. *demography*: ὁ δῆμος + ἡ γραφή =
   "writing" (γράφω) = "the recording
   of information about groups of people," such as statistics on population
   (coined 1880).

4. *endemic*: ἔνδημος, -ον (ἐν + ὁ
   δῆμος) = "among the people,"
   "native," "prevalent among the

people"—ἔνδημα νοσήματα =
"endemic diseases."

5. *epidemic*: ἐπιδημέω (ἐπί + δημο-/ε-)
   "I live among my people," "I live at
   home"; (of diseases) "to be
   widespread" (in Hippocrates).
   There is no adjective ἐπιδημικός,
   -ή, -όν, but the form ἐπιδημιακά
   (νοσήματα) occurs in the Hippo-
   cratic corpus. The word first appears in English in 1603, probably
   borrowed from the French,
   epidémique.

6. *pandemic*: πάνδημος, -ον =
   "belonging to the whole people";
   used of diseases by Galen (second
   century A.D.); *pandemic* is distin-
   guished from *epidemic* as wider in
   effect, i.e., prevalent over a whole
   people or continent.

Grammar 1

Notes:

Exercise 9a

σπεύδοντας . . . βοῶντας . . . ποιοῦντας
   (4–5; masc. acc. pl.), modifying
   τοὺς ἀνθρώπους (4)
βοῶντα (7; masc. acc. sing.), modifying
   ἀλλαντοπώλην (6)
ἐσθίοντες . . . πίνοντες (11; masc. nom.
   pl.), modifying the subject of
   καθίζονται (11)
οὖσαν . . . φέρουσαν (19; fem. acc.
   sing.), modifying εἰκόνα (19)
φέρουσα (28; fem. nom. sing.), modifying ἡ θεός (27)
ἀνέχων (30; masc. nom. sing.), modifying ὁ . . . Φίλιππος (29)
καθορῶντας (35; masc. acc. pl.), modi-
   fyng αὐτούς (35)
ἔχοντα (40; masc. acc. sing.), modifying τὸν πάππον (40)

Exercise 9b

1. οἱ παῖδες τρέχοντες
2. τῷ ἀνδρὶ βαδίζοντι

3.   τοὺς νεανίας τῑμῶντας
4.   τοῖς παισὶν οὖσιν
5.   τῶν νεανιῶν μαχομένων
6.   τὰς γυναῖκας λεγούσᾱς
7.   τὸν Δικαιόπολιν εὐχόμενον
8.   τοῦ δούλου πονοῦντος
9.   αἱ παρθένοι ἀκούουσαι
10. τοῦ ἀγγέλου βοῶντος

Exercise 9c

1. ἄγοντες   The slaves have come leading the oxen.
2. μένοντα   The citizen sees the stranger waiting by the road.
3. θεώμεναι   The women sit in the field watching the children.
4. βάλλοντες The boys don't stop throwing stones.
5. εἰσβαίνουσαν/εἰσερχομένην
            The men watch the girl coming into the temple.

Exercise 9d

1. The children sit in the agora drinking wine.
   οἱ δοῦλοι οἴκαδε σπεύδουσι τοὺς βοῦς ἐλαύνοντες.
2. Do you see the girl hurrying into the temple?
   ὁ ξένος τοὺς παῖδας ὁρᾷ εἰς τὴν ἀγορὰν τρέχοντας.
3. All hear the sausage-seller hawking his wares.
   οὐδεὶς τῆς παρθένου ἀκούει τὴν μητέρα καλούσης.
4. The men leave the women sitting in the house.
   ὁ παῖς τὸν πατέρα εὑρίσκει ἐν τῇ ἀγορᾷ μένοντα.
5. The young man loves the girl who is (being) very beautiful.
   ὁ πατὴρ τὸν παῖδα τῑμᾷ μάλα ἀνδρεῖον ὄντα.

The City of Athens

Illustration (page 102 bottom)

This model of the west side of the agora in the late classical period shows (from left to right) the Tholos, the Metroon (with in front of it the base on which the statues of the eponymous heroes stood), the temple of Apollo Patroos, and the stoa of Zeus. Behind the Metroon is the Bouleuterion. On the hill to the west is the temple of Hephaestus. (American School of Classical Studies at Athens).

Illustration (page 104)

Maidens from the east frieze of the Parthenon (Paris, Louvre).

Illustration (page 105 top)

Model of the Athenian Acropolis as seen from the northwest. This is a plaster copy of the model by G. P. Stevens in the American School of Classical Studies in Athens, with additions by Sylvia Hahn of the Royal Ontario Museum (under supervision of J. W. Grahm) (Toronto, Royal Ontario Museum).

A ramp leads up to the Propylaea (gateway); to the right on a projecting bastion stands the little temple of Athena Nike. Beyond the Propylaea on the right is the sanctuary of Brauronian Artemis. To its left stands the great statue of Athena Promachus. Opposite the Parthenon on the left side of the Acropolis is the Erechtheum.

For further reading, see *The World of Athens*, pp. 78–87.

Η ΠΑΝΗΓΥΡΙΣ (β)

Illustration

Drawn from an Attic red figure cup by the Brygos Painter, ca. 490 B.C. (Würzburg, Museum der Universität). The revel (ὁ κῶμος), involving dancing and drinking in the street, was a regular part of many religious festivals, especially those in honor of Dionysus.

Caption under Illustration

"Many of those who are present, being drunk, are reveling": students will

need help with μεθύοντες and κωμάζουσιν.

Vocabulary

Students may be informed that
ἐπανιέναι is an infinitive corresponding
to the verb ἐπανέρχομαι introduced in the
vocabulary at the beginning of this
chapter; they may recognize the infinitive ἰέναι, which was introduced in vocabulary 7α. Full discussion should be
left until later; the verb εἶμι is treated in
Chapter 17.

Students should see the relationship
between the new nouns τὸ ἱερεῖον and ὁ
ἱερεύς and the noun τὸ ἱερόν in Vocabulary 9α.

Students should note that ἵλαος has
only two sets of forms, one to go with
masculine and feminine nouns and the
other to go with neuter nouns.

Translation

Lines 1–4

Evening is now come. Soon all the
people are silent; for the herald approaches and shouts (says shouting), "Be
silent, citizens; for the procession is approaching. Get out of the way." And so
all get out of the way and wait for the
procession.

Lines 5–11

At that very moment they see the
procession approaching. The heralds
lead; then very beautiful girls walk
(along) carrying baskets full of grapes.
Many citizens carrying skins of wine
follow them and many metics (resident
aliens) carrying trays (of offerings).
Then comes forward the priest of Dionysus and with him noble youths carrying
the statue of Dionysus. Last come attendants leading the sacrificial victims.

[μέτοικοι (8): for this term, see the essay
in Chapter 2.

Word glossed earlier in chapter:
τὴν εἰκόνα the statue.]

Lines 12–16

And so all rejoicing follow the procession toward the sanctuary of the god.

And when they arrive, the priest and the
young men carry the statue of the god
into the temple, and the attendants lead
the victims to the altar. Then the herald
proclaims (proclaiming says) to the people, "Keep holy silence, citizens." And
so the whole crowd is silent and waits
quiet(ly).

[Words glossed earlier in chapter:
τέμενος sanctuary   ὁ ὅμῑλος the
crowd.

εὐφημεῖτε (15): εὐφημέω literally, "I
speak well" = avoid unlucky words,
hence keep holy silence (the safest way
of avoiding unlucky utterance);
εὐφημεῖτε was the traditional call before
any religious ceremony.

ἥσυχος (16): predicate adjective.]

Lines 17–20

And the priest, raising his hands
toward heaven, says, "Lord Dionysus,
listen to my prayer; Thunderer, receive
our sacrifice and be gracious to the people; for you, being gracious (when you
are gracious), keep safe our vines and
make the grapes grow to give us wine."

[Note ὥστε + the infinitive παρέχειν (20,
result clause).]

Lines 21–27

And all those present shout, "eleleu,
iou, iou, Thunderer, be gracious and
make our grapes grow and give us
wine." Then the priest slaughters the
victims; and the attendants, being
ready, take them and cut them up. And
some (parts) they offer to the god, burn-
ing (them) on the altar, and others they
divide up for those present. And when
all is ready, the priest pours wine as a libation and prays to the god. Then all
drink wine and eat the flesh, enjoying
the feast.

[οἱ . . . παρόντες πάντες (21): give help,
if necessary, with the use of the article
with a participle to create a substantive
(formally presented in Grammar 4 later
in this chapter); note the predicate position of πάντες, here following rather than
preceding the article and participle.]

Lines 28–35

It is now midnight, and many of those who are present, being drunk, are reveling. And so Myrrhine, fearing for her children, says, "Come on, husband. Grandfather is very tired; it is time to return to the gates and sleep." But grandfather says, "What are you saying? I am not tired. I want to revel." But Dicaeopolis says, "You are old, father; it's not suitable for you to revel. Come on." So he speaks and leads them toward the gates. And when they arrive, they find the mule, and all sleep on the ground.

[τῶν . . . παρόντων πολλοί (28): give help here as necessary with the partitive genitive, which is presented formally in Grammar 3b later in this chapter.

κωμάζουσιν (29): revels (οἱ κῶμοι) played a regular part in religious celebrations, especially at the festivals of Dionysus; there was dancing and drinking in the streets. These revels were, perhaps, not unlike the carnivals held in Europe before the beginning of Lent.]

Illustration (page 108)

Students should be informed that the remains seen here are from a stone theater built between 342 and 326 B.C. (and modified in Hellenistic and Roman times), replacing the earlier wooden structure.

Word Building

The relationship between the words in the sets is the following. A basic noun or verb is given at the left, from which the stem may be obtained by dropping the endings (-ς, -ς, and -ω). To these stems (note the lengthening of the -ε- of the contract verb) are added the suffix -της, which gives us first declension masculine nouns. Nouns with this suffix describe persons doing something or concerned with something. In the third column, the adjectival suffix -τικος has been added to the stems, producing ad-jectives that denote some relation to the nouns or verbs from which they are formed, often fitness or ability.

1. city; citizen; of or belonging to a citizen (ἡ πολῑτικὴ τέχνη = "the art appropriate to life in the city," "politics").
2. ship; sailor; of or belonging to a ship or a sailor, nautical, naval (τὸ ναυτικόν = "fleet").
3. I make; a maker, poet; capable of making, inventive, poetical.

English derivatives:

πολῑτικός	political
ναυτικός	nautical
ποιητής	poet
ποιητικός	poetic, poetical

Grammar 2

Notes:

Grammar 3

Notes:

Exercise 9e

1. What is the stranger's name?
2. The king is receiving the messenger of the Athenians.
3. We arrive at our father's field.
4. The child walking through the street holds onto his father's hand.
5. The citizens listen to the messenger, wanting to learn the words/proposals of the king.
6. Some of the girls are waiting by the spring, and others are already returning with their mothers.
7. ἀκούομεν τοὺς τοῦ ἀγγέλου λόγους.
8. ἔρχομαι πρὸς τὴν τοῦ ποιητοῦ οἰκίαν.

9. ζητοῦσιν τὸν τῆς παρθένου πατέρα.
10. ἡ μήτηρ ἀκούει τῆς παρθένου δακρῡούσης καὶ σπεύδει ἐκ τῆς οἰκίᾱς.
11. οἱ πολῖται τοῦ ἀγγέλου λαμβάνονται καὶ ἄγουσιν αὐτὸν πρὸς τὸν βασιλέᾱ.
12. τῶν γυναικῶν πολλαὶ βούλονται πρὸς τὸ ἄστυ ἰέναι μετὰ τῶν ἀνδρῶν.

Note ἕχεται with the genitive in no. 4. See Grammar 3d in this chapter.

Grammar 4

Notes:

Exercise 9f

1. The father tells his boy to stay in the house; but he does not obey him.
2. Some of the citizens are going home, others are staying, watching the procession.
3. The girls carrying the baskets are very beautiful.
4. Those who are watching the dances rejoice very much.
5. Do you see the men working in the field?

Ο ΟΔΥΣΣΕΥΣ ΚΑΙ Η ΚΙΡΚΗ

Title: "Odysseus and Circe"

Based on *Odyssey* 10.134–400.

Translation

Lines 1–7
When Aeolus sends us away, we sail away grieving and soon arrive at the island of Aeaea. There lives Circe, who is (being) a terrible goddess.. Leaving my comrades by the ship, I climb a hill, wanting to learn if any man lives on the island. And when I arrive at the top of the hill, I see smoke rising toward heaven. And so I return to the ship and tell some of my companions to stay by the

ship and others to go to the middle of the island and learn who lives there. And Eurylochus leads them.
[Compound verb to be deduced: ἀποπέμπει (1).

We do not gloss Αἰαίᾱν (2) and ἡ Κίρκη (2), since the English equivalents have just occurred in the lead-in.]

Lines 8–14
They find Circe's house (being) in the middle of a woods; and near the house they see many wolves and many lions. Seeing these, they are very afraid and wait at the door. Then they hear Circe singing inside. And so they call her; and she comes out the door and calls them in. And they all follow her; Eurylochus alone stays outside, fearing some danger. Circe leads the others in and tells them to sit (themselves) down and gives them food and wine; but with the food she mixes evil drugs.
[Compound verb to be deduced: εἰσκαλεῖ (11).]

Lines 15–17
And when my comrades eat the food, Circe strikes them with her wand and drives them to the pigsties; and they at once become pigs. Then Circe throws them acorns to eat and leaves them in the sties.

Illustration (page 111)

Detail of an Attic red figure calyx crater by the Persephone painter, ca. 440 B.C. (New York, Metropolitan Museum). Circe drops the drugged cup and runs away, while Odysseus' companions, half transformed into swine, appeal to him for help.

Exercise 9g

1. ἐπεὶ ὁ Εὐρύλοχος ὁρᾷ τί γίγνεται, φεύγει καὶ τρέχει πρὸς τὴν ναῦν.
2. ἐγὼ δέ, ἐπεὶ πάντα ἀκούω, πρὸς τὴν τῆς Κίρκης οἰκίᾱν πορεύομαι/ ἔρχομαι, βουλόμενος τοὺς ἑταίρους σῴζειν.
3. ἡ δὲ Κίρκη σῖτόν τε παρέχει μοι καὶ οἶνον· ἔπειτα δὲ τῷ ῥάβδῳ

τύπτουσά/πλήττουσά με κελεύει εἰς
τοὺς συφεοὺς ἰέναι.
4.   ἐγὼ δὲ σῦς οὐ γίγνομαι· ἡ δὲ μάλα
φοβουμένη ἐθέλει τοὺς ἐμοὺς
ἑταίρους λύειν.

Your students might enjoy reading
or hearing a translation of the whole
story. Circe's charms failed against
Odysseus because on his way to her house
he met a youth, who was Hermes in
disguise; Hermes gave him an antidote,
a good drug, μῶλυ "moly," which pro-
tected him.

10
Η ΣΥΜΦΟΡΑ (α)

Title: "The Misfortune"

Students will need to be given the meaning of the word.

The purposes of this chapter are:

1.   Reading: to conclude the episode of the family's visit to the festival in Athens with a surprise ending that precipitates a new movement of the plot and to conclude the episodes of Odysseus' adventures from the *Odyssey*
2.   Grammar: (α) to present the forms of two more third declension nouns; (β) to present examples of impersonal verbs, to review words used to introduce questions, and to present a consolidation of the forms of λύω, φιλέω, and τῑμάω that have been presented so far in this course
3.   Background: to provide background information on Athenian festivals

Illustration

Drawn from an Attic red figure column crater, ca. 460 B.C. (Basel, Antiken Museum).

Caption under Illustration

"The first chorus comes forward, praising the works of Dionysus": encourage students to deduce the meaning of ὑμνῶν.

Vocabulary

Notes:

Translation

Lines 1–7

The next day as soon as the sun rises, Dicaeopolis wakes his wife, the grandfather, and the children and leads them to the theater of Dionysus. And so they arrive early, but already masses of (very many) people are filling the theater. And so grandfather groans and says, "Oh dear, oh dear! The whole theater is full. Where is it possible to sit?" But Dicaeopolis says, "Cheer up, granddad," and leads them up and finds a bench at the top of the theater.

Lines 8–11

As soon as they sit down, the trumpeter comes forward and blows his trumpet, telling the citizens to keep holy silence. Then the priest of Dionysus approaches the altar and makes a libation, praying to the god; "Lord Dionysus, gracious(ly) receive the libation and, rejoicing, watch the dances."

Lines 12–17

Then the first chorus comes forward into the dancing circle, praising the works of Dionysus. And so Melissa is amazed as she watches and rejoices listening (to their song). So beautifully does the chorus dance. Five choruses of boys and five of men compete in order and all dance very well. And when the tenth chorus ends, the victors (those winning) receive their wreaths and all those present hurry out of the theater.

Word Study

1.   *agonistic:* "competitive," from the root of the verb ἀγωνίζονται that appears in line 15 of passage α in this chapter.
2.   *macroeconomics:* "the study of large scale economic trends," from μακρός "large" + τὰ οἰκονομικά "economics."
3.   *xenophobia:* "fear of strangers," from ὁ ξένος "foreigner" + the root seen in φοβέομαι "I fear."
4.   *pyromaniac:* "one mad about fire," from τὸ πῦρ "fire" + ἡ μανία "madness," "mania."
5.   *ophthalmic:* "concerned with the eyes," from ὁ ὀφθαλμός "eye"; Galen (second century A.D.) uses

the word ὁ ὀφθαλμικός = "ophthalmic surgeon."

Grammar 1

Both πόλις and ἄστυ may mean "city," and both are used in reference to Athens. The word ἄστυ refers to the city as opposed to the country (ἀγρός) or to the city as a collection of buildings as opposed to the city as seen in its body of citizens, the πόλις.

For the irregular accent of πόλεως and πόλεων and for the accusative plural πόλεις (instead of πόλε-ας > πόλης), see Reference Grammar, p. 216.

Exercise 10a

1. We are going to the city, wanting to see both the festival and the procession; do you want to go with us?
2. I very much want to go, but when do you intend to return from the city?
3. We intend to stay the night in the city and to come back tomorrow.
4. We are already at the agora, but there are so many people in the streets that it is scarcely possible to go forward to the Acropolis.
5. For all the citizens are here and all the resident aliens, and many foreigners have come from the cities of the empire.
6. How beautiful the girls are who are carrying the baskets. Do you see the priest and the young men carrying the statue of the god?
7. Now they are entering the sanctuary. Don't you want to follow the procession into the sanctuary?

In no. 1 it may be necessary to remind students about the rules for elision: μετὰ ἡμῶν > μεθ' ἡμῶν. See Chapter 5, Grammar 4, page 45.

Festivals

Illustration (page 114)

From the west frieze of the Parthenon; the cavalry (οἱ ἱππεῖς) gallop up to join the procession (London, British Museum).

Illustration (page 115)

Detail of Attic red figure bell crater, ca. 440 B.C. (Frankfurt, Archäologisches Museum). A statue of the god with laurel branch and bow stands on a column at the right. The priest places the inedible parts of the sacrificed animal on the bloodstained altar. The boy behind the priest carries the edible parts of the animal, wrapped on long spits and ready to be cooked. Note the laurel wreaths.

For further reading, see *the World of Athens*, pp. 118–124.

Η ΣΥΜΦΟΡΑ (β)

Illustration

Drawn from an Attic red figure cup by Epictetus, ca. 520–510 B.C. (Athens, Agora Museum).

Caption under Illustration

"Philip sees some young men fighting in the road."

Vocabulary

The use of the impersonal verbs will be formally presented in Grammar 2; the examples given with the vocabulary entries will help students with the reading.

Translation

Lines 1–8
It is already midday, and Dicaeopolis wants to return to the farm. "Come on," he says, "it's time to hurry home, for we must be there before night." But Myrrhine says, "But, my dear husband, don't you want to watch the tragedies? Can't we return tomorrow?" But Dicaeopolis says, "No, (but) we must go at once. For already we have been away from the farm for a long time, and Xanthias is certainly doing nothing.

the oxen are hungry, the flocks are running off, and the house is probably on
fire. Come on! We must hurry."

[Note that ἄπεσμεν (6) (present tense)
with πολυν χρόνον is most naturally
translated with a present perfect tense in
English, "we have been away . . . for a
long time."]

Lines 9–18
So he says and leads them quickly to
the gates. But while they are hurrying
through the streets, Philip sees some
young men fighting in the road; for they
have drunk lots of (much) wine and are
drunk. And so Philip stays, watching
the fight. And finally the other youths
throw (a certain) one down and don't stop
beating (striking) him. And Philip,
fearing for him, runs to (them) and
says, "Stop, don't beat him, men, for you
are killing the poor man." And one of
the youths, shouting fiercely, turns to
Philip and says, "Who are you to (being
who do you) interfere like this?" And he
hits him. And he falls to the ground and
remains motionless.

[Compound verbs to be deduced:
καταβάλλουσι (13) and προστρέχει (14).]

Lines 19–27
And his parents, hearing the shouts,
hurry to the boy and see him lying on the
ground. And so they lift him up, but he
still remains motionless. And Melissa
says, "Zeus, what's the matter with the
poor boy?" And his mother says, "Carry
him to the spring." And so they carry
him to the spring and pour water over his
head. And soon he moves and recovers.
He gets up and hears his mother talking.
Looking toward her, he says, "Where
are you, mother? Why is it dark?" And
his mother says, "But it's not dark, son,
look here!" But the boy sees nothing; for
he is blind.

[Students should remember τυφλός
"blind" (27) from the Cyclops story in
Chapter 7β.]

Word Building

1. Set 1 consists of primitive verbs and
    nouns formed from a common root:
    I fight: battle
    I pray: prayer
    I wish: will, determination, counsel,
        council, etc.
    I say: word
    I send: procession
    I hasten: haste
    Note the change in the stem vowel or
    diphthong in the last three exam-
    ples; this is regular.
    Sets 2–5 show denominative verbs
    formed by the addition of a suffix to a
    noun stem.

2. Suffix -άω/-άομαι
    sight: I watch
    shout: I shout
    victory: I defeat, win
    silence: I am silent

3. Suffix -έω/-έομαι; note the change
    from νοσο- (noun) to νοσε- (verb):
    wise: I am wise
    sickness: I am sick
    fear: I fear

4. Suffix -εύω; this suffix was derived
    from nouns with stems ending in
    -ευ- and then extended to other
    stems:
    king: I am king
    citizen: I am a citizen
    danger: I am in danger
    child: I educate

5. Suffix -ίζω/-ίζομαι
    time: I spend time, tarry
    calculation: I calculate
    anger: I am angry

Grammar 2

Notes:

Exercise 10b

1. It is time to return; we must set out at
    once.
    μὴ ἐνταῦθα μένετε· δεῖ ἡμᾶς
    σπεύδειν.

2. Can't we/may we not watch the
    tragedies?
    ἆρ᾽ οὐκ ἔξεστί μοι ἐν τῷ ἄστει
    μένειν;
3. You must not strike the young man.
    δεῖ ἡμᾶς φέρειν τὸν παῖδα πρὸς τὴν
    κρήνην.
4. Philip must obey his father.
    δεῖ τὴν Μέλιτταν οἴκοι μένειν.
5. May I learn (am I allowed to learn)
    what is the matter with the boy?
    ἔξεστιν ἡμῖν πρὸς τὸ ἄστυ
    πορεύεσθαι· δεῖ εὐθὺς ὁρμᾶσθαι.

Grammar 3

Notes:

Exericse 10c

1. Why does Odysseus want to sail to
    the island?
2. He wants to learn who lives on the
    island.
3. The Cyclops asks Odysseus from
    where he has come.
4. How do Odysseus and his comrades
    escape?
5. Does Odysseus save all his com-
    rades?
6. When Odysseus escapes, where
    does he sail to?
7. Aeolus asks Odysseus who he is
    and where he has come from.
8. Aeolus asks Odysseus when he in-
    tends to sail.

Grammar 4

Notes:

Ο ΟΔΥΣΣΕΥΣ
ΤΟΥΣ ΕΤΑΙΡΟΥΣ
ΑΠΟΛΛΥΣΙΝ

Title: "Odysseus Loses His Comrades"

Supply the meaning of the verb. The
story is based on *Odyssey* 12.165–425.

Translation

Lines 1–7
    Odysseus still suffers many terrible
things while striving (hastening) to return to his fatherland. For he scarcely
escapes the Sirens, and sailing along
Sicily he gets (falls) into the greatest
danger. For on one side is Scylla, a terrible monster, which has (having) six
heads, which rushing out of a cave seizes
those sailing past and eats (them); and
on the other side is Charybdis, a very
terrifying whirlpool, which swallows
down everything. And Odysseus, fleeing from Charybdis, sails past Scylla.
And rushing out of her cave she seizes
six of his comrades; but the others
Odysseus saves.

[ἐμπίπτει (3): students are to recall this
word from Chapter 7α:12 or to deduce its
meaning (= ἐν + πίπτει).
    Compound verbs to be deduced:
παραπλέοντας (4) and παραπλεῖ (6).
Students will get the meaning of παρά
from the prepositional phrase παρὰ τὴν
Σικελίαν, glossed in line 2.]

Lines 8–13
    Soon they arrive at another island;
and there they find many oxen; his
comrades want to kill and eat them. But
Odysseus says, "Don't harm the oxen;
for they belong to the Sun." But they do
not obey him but kill the oxen. And so
the Sun, praying to his father, Zeus, says,
"Father Zeus, the comrades of Odysseus
are killing my oxen. And so punish
them; if not, I shall never shine among
men again."

Lines 14–17
    And Zeus hears his prayer (him
praying); for when Odysseus and his
comrades, sailing away, leave the island, he sends a terrible storm and
strikes the ship with a thunderbolt. And
so all his comrades fall out of the ship
and die; and Odysseus alone escapes,
holding onto the mast.

[Compound verb to be deduced:
ἐκπίπτουσι (16).]

Illustration (page 122)

From a stamnos by the Siren
Painter, ca. 475 B.C. (London, British
Museum). The crew have bound
Odysseus to the mast, on his orders, so
that he can hear the singing of the Sirens
but not try to reach them. Odysseus' crew
can hear nothing, since their ears have
been plugged with wax.

Exercise 10d

1. ἐννέα μὲν ἡμέρᾱς ὁ ἄνεμος τὸν Ὀ-
    δυσσέᾱ φέρει διὰ τῆς θαλάττης, τῇ
    δὲ δεκάτῃ εἰς ἄλλην τινὰ νῆσον
    ἀφικνεῖται.

2. ἐκεῖ δὲ οἰκεῖ ἡ νύμφη Καλυψώ·
    εὐμενῶς δὲ αὐτὸν δέχεται.

3. φιλοῦσα αὐτόν, "μένε μετά μου
    αἰεί," φησίν, "ἐν τῇ νήσῳ." ὁ δὲ Ὀ-
    δυσσεὺς βούλεται (οἴκαδε) νοστεῖν
    καὶ τήν τε γυναῖκα ὁρᾶν καὶ τὸν
    παῖδα.

4. τέλος δὲ ὁ Ζεὺς ἄγγελον πέμπει καὶ
    τὴν νύμφην κελεύει τὸν Ὀδυσσέᾱ
    λῦειν.

5. ἡ Καλυψὼ κελεύει αὐτὸν σχεδίᾱν
    ποιεῖν καὶ βοηθεῖ αὐτῷ.

6. ἐπεὶ δὲ ἑτοίμη ἐστὶν ἡ σχεδίᾱ, ὁ Ὀ-
    δυσσεὺς ἀποπλεῖ χαίρων.

PREVIEW OF NEW VERB FORMS

This page of the student's book sets forth some of the most basic information about the formation of the future, imperfect, aorist, and perfect tenses. Familiarity with this basic information will help students recognize and understand new verb forms as they meet them in the readings in the following chapters. Concentrate on the imperfect and the first and second aorists. These tenses will be formally introduced in Chapters 11–13. Some verbs in the future and the perfect tenses will appear in the readings in Chapters 11–16, but these tenses will not be formally introduced until the second half of the course, in Book II.

The summary of tense formation given here is necessarily incomplete; it does not mention, for example, temporal (as opposed to syllabic) augment. Concentrate on the main points, as spelled out in notes 1–5 at the bottom of the Preview page.

Below and on the next two pages we give charts of the verb εἰμί, of λύω, and of the three types of contract verbs. These may be duplicated and distributed to students. They may also be enlarged and displayed prominently in the classroom. The charts encourage comparison between the different sets of forms. For example, the imperfect of λύω and the second aorist of λαμβάνω are presented side-by-side so that the similarities of the endings are readily apparent. In teaching these new verb forms emphasize both the features that distinguish one set from others, e.g., the -σα of the first aorist, but also emphasize the similarities, e.g., the endings of the imperfect and those of the second aorist (mentioned above) and the endings of the present imperative, infinitive, and participle of λύω and those of the second aorist imperative, infinitive, and participle of λαμβάνω.

PRESENT	IMPERFECT
Indicative	
εἰμί	ἦν
εἶ	ἦσθα
ἐστί(ν)	ἦν
ἐσμέν	ἦμεν
ἐστέ	ἦτε
εἰσί(ν)	ἦσαν
Imperative	
ἴσθι	
ἔστε	
Infinitive	
εἶναι	
Participle	
ὤν, οὖσα, ὄν	

Active Voice

PRESENT	IMPERFECT	2ND AORIST	1ST AORIST
Indicative			
λύω	ἔλῡον	ἔλαβον	ἔλῡσα
λύεις	ἔλῡες	ἔλαβες	ἔλῡσας
λύει	ἔλῡε(ν)	ἔλαβε(ν)	ἔλῡσε(ν)
λύομεν	ἐλύομεν	ἐλάβομεν	ἐλύσαμεν
λύετε	ἐλύετε	ἐλάβετε	ἐλύσατε
λύουσι(ν)	ἔλῡον	ἔλαβον	ἔλῡσαν
Imperative			
λῦε		λαβέ	λῦσον
λύετε		λαβέτε	λύσατε
Infinitive			
λύειν		λαβεῖν	λῦσαι
Participle			
λύων, λύουσα, λῦον		λαβών, λαβοῦσα, λαβόν	λύσᾱς, λύσᾱσα, λῦσαν

Middle Voice

PRESENT	IMPERFECT	2ND AORIST	1ST AORIST
Indicative			
λύομαι	ἐλῡόμην	ἐγενόμην	ἐλῡσάμην
λύῃ *or* λύει	ἐλύου	ἐγένου	ἐλύσω
λύεται	ἐλύετο	ἐγένετο	ἐλύσατο
λῡόμεθα	ἐλῡόμεθα	ἐγενόμεθα	ἐλῡσάμεθα
λύεσθε	ἐλύεσθε	ἐγένεσθε	ἐλύσασθε
λύονται	ἐλύοντο	ἐγένοντο	ἐλύσαντο
Imperative			
λύου		γενοῦ	λῦσαι
λύεσθε		γένεσθε	λύσασθε
Infinitive			
λύεσθαι		γενέσθαι	λύσασθαι
Participle			
λῡόμενος, -η, -ον		γενόμενος, -η, -ον	λῡσάμενος, -η, -ον

Active Voice

PRESENT	IMPERF.	PRESENT	IMPERF.	PRESENT	IMPERF.
Indicative					
φιλῶ	ἐφίλουν	τῑμῶ	ἐτῑ́μων	δηλῶ	ἐδήλουν
φιλεῖς	ἐφίλεις	τῑμᾷς	ἐτῑ́μᾱς	δηλοῖς	ἐδήλους
φιλεῖ	ἐφίλει	τῑμᾷ	ἐτῑ́μᾱ	δηλοῖ	ἐδήλου
φιλοῦμεν	ἐφιλοῦμεν	τῑμῶμεν	ἐτῑμῶμεν	δηλοῦμεν	ἐδηλοῦμεν
φιλεῖτε	ἐφιλεῖτε	τῑμᾶτε	ἐτῑμᾶτε	δηλοῦτε	ἐδηλοῦτε
φιλοῦσι(ν)	ἐφίλουν	τῑμῶσι(ν)	ἐτῑ́μων	δηλοῦσι(ν)	ἐδήλουν
Imperative					
φίλει		τῑ́μᾱ		δήλου	
φιλεῖτε		τῑμᾶτε		δηλοῦτε	
Infinitive					
φιλεῖν		τῑμᾶν		δηλοῦν	
Participle					
φιλῶν, φιλοῦσα, φιλοῦν		τῑμῶν, τῑμῶσα, τῑμῶν		δηλῶν, δηλοῦσα, δηλοῦν	

Middle Voice

PRESENT	IMPERF.	PRESENT	IMPERF.	PRESENT	IMPERF.
Indicative					
φιλοῦμαι	ἐφιλούμην	τῑμῶμαι	ἐτῑμώμην	δηλοῦμαι	ἐδηλούμην
φιλῇ *or* φιλεῖ	ἐφιλοῦ	τῑμᾷ	ἐτῑμῶ	δηλοῖ	ἐδηλοῦ
φιλεῖται	ἐφιλεῖτο	τῑμᾶται	ἐτῑμᾶτο	δηλοῦται	ἐδηλοῦτο
φιλούμεθα	ἐφιλούμεθα	τῑμώμεθα	ἐτῑμώμεθα	δηλούμεθα	ἐδηλύμεθα
φιλεῖσθε	ἐφιλεῖσθε	τῑμᾶσθε	ἐτῑμᾶσθε	δηλοῦσθε	ἐδηλοῦσθε
φιλοῦνται	ἐφιλοῦντο	τῑμῶνται	ἐτῑμῶντο	δηλοῦνται	ἐδηλοῦντο
Imperative					
φιλοῦ		τῑμῶ		δηλοῦ	
φιλεῖσθε		τῑμᾶσθε		δηλοῦσθε	
Infinitive					
φιλεῖσθαι		τῑμᾶσθαι		δηλοῦσθαι	
Participle					
φιλούμενος, -η, -ον		τῑμώμενος, -η, -ον		δηλούμενος, -η, -ον	

11

Ο ΙΑΤΡΟΣ (α)

Title: "The Doctor"

Students will find the word in the vocabulary list.

The purposes of this chapter are:

1. Reading: to continue the story from the new turn it takes with the blinding of Philip (the family returns to the house of Dicaeopolis's brother, and the next day they visit a doctor); to begin a set of readings from Herodotus at the end of this and subsequent chapters, with the story of Democedes' cure of King Darius (theme of medicine)
2. Grammar: (α and β) to introduce past tenses of the verb, beginning with the relatively uncomplicated second aorist
3. Background: to provide background information on Greek medicine

Caption under Illustration

"When they arrived at the house of his brother, Dicaeopolis knocked on the door": encourage students to recognize ἀφίκοντο as an aorist by having them look closely at the stem and observing that the ν of the present stem is no longer there (remind students about the change of the stem when going from present to second aorist; see Preview of New Verb Forms, page 123). The new words τοῦ ἀδελφοῦ and ἔκοψε are in the vocabulary list, but students should be encouraged to deduce the meaning of the verb with the help of a comprehension question ("What did Dicaeopolis do when he arrived at his brother's house?"). Do not dwell on the form of the first aorist ἔκοψε at this stage. If students are curious about it, simply point out the augment and the σ concealed in the ψ. The form will appear (unglossed) in the readings (11α:8 and 11β:9 and 10).

Vocabulary

We repeat ἀφικνέομαι, γίγνομαι, λαμβάνω, and πάσχει in this vocabulary list in order to show their aorists. Likewise, we give the compound εἰσάγω. Point out the changes in the stems and have students translate the aorist forms. Students will then be ready to recognize the aorists ἔμαθεν (1), ἔπαθεν (15, 20), ἐγένετο (16), and εἰσήγαγεν (17) without the help of glosses. Concentrate on these forms (augment + second aorist stem + ending). Students have already met the aorist ἀφίκοντο in the caption.

We also give the aorist of κόπτω since this verb is used in the aorist in the caption and in the readings (11α:8 and 11β:9 and 10).

The preposition παρά has the meaning "to" with the accusative (see lines 3–4), most commonly with persons, not places.

Verbs

Reading passage α contains the following second aorist verbs and participles: ἔμαθεν (1), ἀφίκοντο (8), ἐλθών (9), ἰδών (10), εἴπετε (11), ἰδών (15), ἔπαθεν (15), εἰσέλθετε (16), εἴπετε (16), ἐγένετο (16), εἰπών (17), εἰσήγαγεν (17), γενόμενα (18), εἶπον (18), ἐλθέ (18), ἔπαθεν (20), ἐλθέ (21), and εἰσελθόντες (22). The forms that have not appeared in vocabulary lists are glossed at their first occurrence. The forms in boldface in the list above should be highlighted in teaching this passage, and they are treated in the grammar immediately following. The other forms (imperatives and participles of ἔρχομαι, ὁράω, and λέγω) may be left for full discussion until after Grammar 5, where these forms are presented. From the Preview of New Verb Forms students will be able to see for themselves how the aorists of μάνθανω and πάσχω are formed; from the vocabulary list they will see that ἀφικνέομαι/ἀφῖκόμην and γίγνομαι/ ἐγενόμην also show changes in their stems from present to aorist.

The perfect tense γέγονεν (14, 20) will be recognized by students from what they learned in the Preview of New Verb Forms; it need not be discussed further at this stage.

The one future tense, κομιῶ (25), is formed without a σ but is glossed and need not be discussed at this stage.

Translation

Lines 1–6

But when Myrrhine learned that the child was blind, in tears (crying) she said to her husband, "Oh, Zeus, what should we do? Pray to the gods to help us." But Dicaeopolis said, "But we must take the boy to a doctor. But evening is falling already. And so now (we) must hurry to my brother's house and ask him to receive us. And tomorrow (we) must look for a doctor.

[With impersonal verbs the person may be expressed in the accusative, e.g., "τί δεῖ ἡμᾶς ποιεῖν;" (2) = "What should (must) we do?" It is very common, however, to leave the person unexpressed, as we do in lines 4 and 6.]

Lines 7–16

And so leading the boy they walk slowly to the brother's house. And when they arrived, Dicaeopolis knocked on the door. And his brother, coming to the door and seeing Dicaeopolis, said, "Greetings, brother! How are you? And Myrrhine, greetings to you, too. But tell me, what's the matter with you? Why aren't you returning to the country but are still staying in the city? For evening is already falling." And Dicaeopolis (replied), "I am well, but the boy—look! he is (has become) blind. He sees nothing. And so we are here asking you to receive us." And his brother seeing that the boy was blind (the boy being blind), said, "Zeus, whatever happened to the boy (whatever did the boy suffer)? Come in and tell me what happened."

[βαδίζουσιν (7): to avoid introducing too many examples of tenses that have not been formally presented, in this and the following chapter we make use of the historic present. Students may be told that Greek authors often use the historic present in past narrative to make the action more vivid.

τί ποτε (15): it is an odd fact of language that ποτε is used in Greek to intensify an interrogative, just like *ever* in English.]

Lines 17–25

So saying he led them into the house, and they told him all that had happened. And he, calling his wife, said, "Come here. For Dicaeopolis and Myrrhine are here; and a terrible thing has happened to Philip (Philip suffered a terrible thing); for he has become blind. And so take him and the women to the women's quarters. And you, brother, come here." And so Dicaeopolis and his brother, going into the men's quarters, have a long discussion (talk about many things), considering what they should do. Finally, his brother said, "Enough (of) words. I know a good (wise, clever) doctor and tomorrow, if you agree (if it seems good to you), I will take you to him. But now—for it's late—we must sleep."

[πολλὰ διαλέγονται (22–23): the *internal accusative*, "they talk many things," can often be better translated somewhat freely in English, e.g., "they have a long discussion."]

Word Study

1. *logic*: ὁ λόγος. Among its other meanings (which cover six columns in Liddell and Scott's *Lexicon*) are "reflection," "reasoning," and "reason" (as a faculty). λογικός, -ή, -όν, from which *logic* is directly derived, can mean "intellectual," "dialectical," and, finally, "logical." ἡ λογικὴ (τεχνή), on which several Greek philosophers wrote treatises, = "logic."

2. *dialogue*: from διαλέγομαι = "I talk," "I have a conversation" is formed ὁ διάλογος.
3. *monologue*: μόνος + ὁ λόγος, coined in English on the analogy of *dialogue*; no such Greek word.
4. *prologue*: ὁ πρόλογος. πρό = before + λόγος, used in Greek of the prologue of a tragedy.
5. *eulogy*: ἡ εὐλογία. εὖ + λόγος, λέγω—"speaking well of," "praise," "eulogy."

Grammar 1

Note that on page 127 we do not give the emphatic translations, "I did take," "I did become," but teachers should remind students of these possibilities.

Point out the thematic or variable vowels in the sets of forms on page 127.

While the endings of the imperative, infinitive, and participle are the same in the second aorist as in the present, students should note the different accents on the aorist active infinitive and participle: λαβεῖν (instead of present λαμβάνειν) and λαβών, λαβοῦσα, λαβόν (instead of present λαμβάνων, λαμβάνουσα, λαμβάνον).

The accent of the second aorist active imperative is usually recessive, as in the present tense, e.g., λεῖπε/λείπετε and λίπε/λίπετε. The second aorist active imperative of λαμβάνω is an exception: λαβέ/λάβετε. See Grammar 5.

Exercise 11a

ἔπαθεν (15, 20); ἐγένετο (16) and γενόμενα (18)

Exercise 11b

Sets of forms of this sort are not provided in this handbook; teachers should check students' work carefully.

Exercise 11c

Sets of forms of this sort are not provided in this handbook; teachers should check students' work carefully.

Grammar 2 and 3

Notes:

Grammar 4

Students should be required to learn the second aorists given in this list thoroughly; they should be able to recite and write from memory the present, the aorist indicative, and the aorist participle.

Exercise 11d

1. The woman, learning that her boy became blind, said to her husband, "Zeus, what must we do?"
2. Arriving at the brother's house, they told him what had happened to the boy (what the boy had suffered).
3. The men, leaving the women in the house, led the child to the doctor.
4. The farmer, having led the (his) dog to the mountain, found the wolf about to attack (fall upon) the flocks.
5. The mother, having given food to the boy, tells him to hurry to the field.
6. Arriving at the field he gave his father the dinner.
7. The father, leaving the plow in the field, took the dinner.
8. The boy pelted the wolf, and it fled in fear (fearing).
9. The young men died fighting for their city.
10. (Although) suffering terribly (terrible things), they did not flee but fell fighting bravely.

In no. 2 students may translate "they told him what happened," but strictly speaking the aorist indicates time prior to that of the main verb, which is here in the past tense (εἶπον), and so the pluperfect should be used in English ("had happened").

In no. 5, give help as needed with παρασχοῦσα: be sure students see that this comes from παρέχω.

Greek Medicine

Illustration (page 130)

Marble relief from Oropos, ca. 370 B.C. (Athens, National Archaeological Museum). Note the all-seeing eyes of the god at the top of the relief.

For further reading, see *The World of Athens*, pp. 190–192, 278–283, and 296–297, and *The Oxford History of the Classical World*, pp. 230–232.

Ο ΙΑΤΡΟΣ (β)

Illustration

Drawn from an East Greek gravestone, ca 500 B.C. (Basel, Antikenmuseum).

Caption under Illustration

"The doctor said, "Come here, boy. What happened to you? How did you become blind?" The second aorists ἔπαθες and ἐγένου reinforce the grammar in the first half of this chapter; ἐλθέ has been familiar as a vocabulary item since Chapter 2 and will appear in the grammatical discussion in the second half of this chapter.

Vocabulary

Note that in this and subsequent vocabulary lists forms of the aorist participle as well as the indicative will be given; this is to remind students that the augment occurs only in the indicative and to display a typical unaugmented aorist form, since the unaugmented forms will be met frequently in the readings.

Note also that we repeat the entries for ἔρχομαι, λέγω, and ὁράω here to show their aorists; familiarity with the aorists of these verbs will help students with the reading passage.

ἡ δραχμή and ὁ ὀβολός: there were six obols to a drachma (6,000 drachmas to a talent, the largest monetary unit). With regard to purchasing power, in the time of Pericles, a workman received one drachma a day, and a juryman received two obols, from which we may deduce that a drachma a day would support a family and two obols a single person. Coins, all silver in the fifth century, ranged from a quarter obol to tetradrachma pieces.

The entry for πρός is repeated here with the new meaning "against" (see lines 3–4).

Verbs

Reading passage β contains the following second aorist verbs and participles; the examples in this list that are not in boldface are forms that the student should be able to identify from the grammatical material in the first half of this chapter; the forms in boldface are treated in the grammar in the second half of the chapter: ἐγένετο (1), λιπόντες (2), ἤγαγον (3), ἐλάβετο (3), κατέπεσεν (4), ἀφίκοντο (5), **ἐλθέ** (7), **εἰπών** (7), **ἐπανῆλθεν** (8), **προσελθών** (9), **ἦλθεν** (10), **ἐξελθών** (10), **εἰπών** (15), παρέσχεν (16), **ἐξελθών** (19), **εἰσέλθετε** (19), **εἶδεν** (21), **προσελθών** (21), ἔπαθεν (23), **ἐλθέ** (23), ἔπαθες (24), ἐγένου (24), **εἶπεν** (25), ἀφικόμενος (34), γενόμενα (34), **εἶπεν** (35), μαθοῦσα (35), παρασχεῖν (39), **ἐλθών** (42), ἐξεῖλε (42), and παρέσχεν (42).

Translation

Lines 1–8

The next day when day first dawned, Dicaeopolis and his brother having left the women in the house led Philip into the road. He took hold of his father's hand, but nevertheless, stumbling against the stones, he fell to the ground. And so his father lifts and carries (him). And so going like this, they soon arrived at the doctor's house. And his brother said, "Look! We have come to the doctor's. Come here and knock (on) the door." After saying this the brother returned home.

Lines 9–17

And so Dicaeopolis going up knocked on the door, but no one came. But when he knocked again, a slave coming out said, "Go to the crows. Who are you to knock on the door (being who do you knock on the door)?" And Dicaeopolis (said), "But, my dear fellow, I am Dicaeopolis, and I am bringing my son to your master; for he has become (is) blind." But the slave (said), "He's busy (he doesn't have leisure)." And Dicaeopolis (said), "But nevertheless, call him. For a terrible thing has happened to the child. But wait, friend." And so saying he gave the slave two obols. And he (replied), "Wait here then. For I will call my master, in case (if perhaps) he is willing to receive you."

[Let students deduce ἐξελθών (10).

Word glossed earlier in chapter: γέγονεν has become, is.

The verb "to be" is frequently omitted in Greek, as in οὐ σχολὴ αὐτῷ, "he doesn't have leisure" (13).]

Lines 18–32

And so father and child wait some little time at the door. Then the slave, coming out, said, "Come in; for my master is willing to receive you." And so the father, leading the boy in, saw the doctor sitting in the courtyard. And so approaching (him) he said, "Greetings. I am Dicaeopolis from Cholleidae, and I am bringing my son to you; for a terrible thing happened to him; he has become (is) blind." And the doctor said, "Come here, boy. What happened to you? How did you become blind?" And so Dicaeopolis told the doctor everything, and he (i.e., the doctor) examines the boy's eyes for a long time. And finally (he said) "I cannot help him. For the eyes are not diseased at all. And so men cannot help, but for the gods all things

are possible. And so you must take the boy to Epidaurus and pray to Asclepius, in case he is willing to heal him." And Dicaeopolis (said), "Alas! (for) how can I, a poor man, (being poor) go to Epidaurus?" But the doctor said, "That's your business, my man. Goodbye."

[Words glossed earlier in chapter: εἰσέλθετε come in! γέγονεν has become, is.

Compound verb to be deduced: εἰσηγούμενος (20).

οὐδὲν γὰρ νοσοῦσιν οἱ ὀφθαλμοί (26–27): students should become aware of the use of οὐδέν as an internal accusative, "not at all."]

Lines 33–40

And Dicaeopolis, grieving deeply (much), walks to the door and leads the boy home. And when he arrived (having arrived) he told his brother all that had happened. And Myrrhine, learning everything, (said), "All right (so be it); we cannot fight against necessity. You must take the boy to Epidaurus." But Dicaeopolis said, "But, wife, how can I take the boy there? For we must go by sea; the boy can't go on foot when he's blind. And then how can I give the fare to the ship's captain? For I haven't got the money."

Lines 41–46

But his brother said, "Don't worry, friend." And going to the chest he took out five drachmas and gave (them) to Dicaeopolis. And he receives the money, and, being deeply grateful (having great gratitude), he said, "Oh dearest of men, I pray the gods to give all good things to you who are so kind." And so they decide to hurry the next day to the Piraeus and to look for a ship that is about to sail to Epidaurus.

[Help students as necessary with ἐξεῖλε (42).]

Word Building

1. I live, dwell; dweller, inhabitant; dwelling, house; dwelling, place, room

2. I learn; learner, pupil; act of learning; that which is learned, learning, knowledge

Grammar 5

In discussing the irregular second aorists, it may be useful to go back through the second and third paragraphs of passage α and note the occurrences of indicative, imperative, and participial forms of these verbs. There are ten, if one includes the forms compounded with εἰσ-. Be sure that students recognize these forms as second aorists and understand that the augment occurs only in the indicative forms. Examination of these forms in the context of the reading passage presents an excellent opportunity to stress the concept of *aspect* and the fact that the unaugmented forms usually refer simply to performance of the action itself as a simple event (see Grammar 2).

Grammar 6

In addition to the regular augments as given here, students will meet εἶχε (imperfect of ἔχω) and εἰργάζοντο (imperfect of ἐργάζομαι) in 14α:4 and Exercise 16b, no. 9 (occurrences will be mentioned in the teacher's notes). Perhaps the most common such augment is of the aorist stem ἑλ- (aorist of αἱρέω), which gives the aorist indicative εἷλον (see Grammar 5, page 135, top). Another irregular augment is of the aorist stem ἰδ- (ὁράω), which gives εἶδον (also see Grammar 5, page 135, top). Further examples: ἕπομαι, imperfect εἱπόμην, and ἕλκω, imperfect εἷλκον. These irregularities are noted in the entries in the Greek to English Vocabulary.

Exercise 11e

1. ἐκελευ-. 2. ἠθελ-. 3. ὠτρῦν-. 4. ἰᾱτρευ-. 5. ἠρχ-. 6. ἐλαβ-. 7. ἠγε-. 8. ἠμῡν-. 9. ηὐχ-. 10. ὠνομαζ-. 11. ἠλθ-. 12. ἐμαθ-.

Exercise 11f

1. ἐλάβομεν. 2. ἔμαθε. 3. ἔπαθον. 4. ἔλιπες. 5. πεσών. 6. ἐγενόμεθα. 7. εἰπέ. 8. ἔσχες. 9. ἀφικέσθαι. 10. λιπεῖν. 11. λαβοῦσα. 12. ἐλίπετε/λίπετε. 13. εἰπεῖν. 14. ἦλθον. 15. ἰδεῖν. 16. εἴπομεν. 17. εἶδε(ν). 18. ἐλθεῖν

Students should give translations of both the present tense forms in the book and the aorist forms that they produce.

Exercise 11g

1. The farmer coming into the field saw his daughter sitting under the tree.
2. And so he went up to her and said, "Why are you sitting under the tree weeping, daughter?
3. And she said, "Bringing you your dinner, father, I fell down in the road and hurt my foot.
4. And he said, "Come here, daughter, I must look at your foot."
5. And so he looks at her foot and after seeing that it was not at all bad (sick), he said, "Cheer up, daughter, you've suffered no damage (nothing). And so give me my dinner and return home."
6. And so the girl having given her father his dinner slowly went away to her home.

Exercise 11h

1. πῶς τυφλὸς ἐγένου, ὦ παῖ; εἰπέ μοι τί ἐγένετο.
2. ποῦ εἶδες τοὺς βοῦς; ἆρ' ἔλιπες αὐτοὺς ἐν τῷ ἀγρῷ;
3. πολλὰ κατὰ θάλατταν παθόντες, τέλος εἰς τὴν γῆν ἀφίκοντο.
4. τοὺς χοροὺς ἰδόντες οἱ παῖδες οἴκαδε ἦλθον καὶ τῷ πατρὶ εἶπον τί ἐγένετο.
5. εἰς τὴν θάλατταν πεσοῦσαι αἱ παρθένοι δεινὰ ἔπαθον.

Students should be warned not to translate "after" in nos. 3 and 4 with a separate word but to let the participles do the job.

Ο ΔΗΜΟΚΗΔΗΣ
ΤΟΝ ΒΑΣΙΛΕΑ
ΙΑΤΡΕΥΕΙ

Title: "Democedes Heals the King"

Students should be able to deduce the meaning of the verb from the noun ἰᾱτρός, which they have had.

You may like to explain to your students before they read this piece that Polycrates, the powerful tyrant of Samos, at whose court Democedes served, was in 522 B.C. lured to the mainland by the Persian governor of Lydia and executed by crucifixion.

Verbs

This reading passage contains the following verbs in the first aorist, which will be treated in the next chapter: ἐκόμισαν (2), ἔβλαψεν (3), ἐκέλευσε (5), ἐθαύμασε (7), and ἰᾱτρευσεν (9). These forms are all glossed here. Students can recognize most of them from what they have learned about the formation of the first aorist in the Preview of New Verb Forms. It will be useful to explain that the ending in the third person singular is -σε(ν) and that π + σ > ψ in ἔβλαψεν.

There are two imperfects: ἐδύναντο (4) and ἐτῑμᾱ (10).

Translation

Lines 1–10
When Polycrates died, the Persians, taking both the other servants of Polycrates and Democedes (=the servants of P. including Democedes), brought them to Susa. And soon a bad thing happened to the king; for falling from his horse he hurt his foot. And the doctors could not help him. But learning that there was a Greek doctor among the slaves, he or-

dered his servants to lead Democedes to him. And so Democedes came into the middle (of the court), dragging fetters and dressed in rags. And so the king seeing him was amazed and asked if he could heal his foot. But Democedes being afraid said that he was not a good (clever) doctor but was willing to try. Then using Greek healing (methods) he quickly healed the foot. And so he became a friend to the king, and he gave him much money and honored (was honoring) him greatly.

[Word glossed earlier in chapter: δύναται is able.

"And so the king seeing him was amazed and asked (ἤρετο) if he could (δύναται) heal his foot": note that the original present tense is kept in the indirect statement in secondary sequence in Greek, while English changes to "could." There is no need to digress on these points at this time; students will write similar sentences in Exercise 11i, nos. 2 and 5 below, but with help from glosses.

Let students deduce the meaning of the verb ἰᾱτρευσεν (9).]

Exercise 11i

1. ἐπεὶ ὁ βασιλεὺς ἔπεσεν ἀπὸ τοῦ ἵππου, κακόν τι ἔπαθεν· οἱ δὲ ἰᾱτροὶ εἶπον ὅτι οὐ δύνανται αὐτὸν ὠφελεῖν.
2. μαθόντες ὅτι ἄλλος τις ἰᾱτρὸς πάρεστιν ἐν τοῖς δούλοις, οἱ θεράποντες εἶπον, "δεῖ τοῦτον τὸν ἰᾱτρὸν παρά σε κομίζειν."
3. ἐπεὶ δὲ ἀφίκετο ὁ ἰᾱτρός, ὁ βασιλεύς, "ἆρα δυνατόν ἐστιν," ἔφη, "τὸν πόδα ἰᾱτρεύειν;"
4. ὁ ἰᾱτρὸς εἶπεν ὅτι ἐθέλει πειρᾶσθαι.
5. ἐπεὶ δὲ ὁ ἰᾱτρὸς τὸν πόδα ἰᾱτρευσεν, ὁ βασιλεὺς μάλα φίλος αὐτῷ ἐγένετο.

12
ΠΡΟΣ ΤΟΝ ΠΕΙΡΑΙΑ
(α)

Title: "To the Piraeus"

The purposes of this chapter are:

1. Reading: (α and β) to record the family's trip to the Piraeus and their negotiations for the voyage to Epidaurus; to continue the readings from Herodotus with the story of Colaeus' voyage beyond the Pillars of Hercules (themes of seafaring and trade)
2. Grammar: (α) to present the forms of the first aorist of λύω, of verbs with stems ending in consonants (other than liquids) and of contract verbs and to present the imperfect of εἰμί; (β) to present the first aorist of verbs with stems ending in liquids and to show how compound verbs are augmented
3. Background: to present a discussion of seafaring and trade in the ancient Mediterranean to accompany the Greek narrative of the voyage to Epidaurus

Illustration

Detail from a black figure cup in Attic style, sixth century B.C. (Paris, Louvre).

Caption under Illustration

"A man approached driving a wagon": from the Preview of New Verb Forms and from the first aorist verbs in the reading at the end of Chapter 11, students should be able to recognize the first aorist προσεχώρησεν; they will deduce ἄμαξαν from the illustration.

Vocabulary

As a further preview of the formation of the first aorist, we give the aorist indicative and participle forms of the new verbs in the vocabulary list. Brief discussion of these forms in the vocabulary list will help students recognize the first aorists in the reading.

Verbs

Highlight the first aorists and the imperfect of the verb "to be" when teaching passage α.

Reading passage α contains the following verbs and participles in the first aorist (discussed in the grammar sections following the reading) and the following forms of the imperfect of εἰμί and its compounds (also presented in the following grammar section) (help with some, but not all, of these aorists and imperfects is given in the glosses): ἐκέλευσε (2), παρεσκευάσαντο (3), ἦσαν (4), ἠθέλησε (4), ἦν (5), βαδίσᾱσα (6), ἦν (6), ἔδοξεν (6), παρῆσαν (7), ἡγησάμενος (8), προσεχώρησε (9), ποιησάμενος (9), ηὔξατο (9), κελεύσαντες (11), ὥρμησαν (12), ἦν (13), ἐνῆσαν (14), ἔπταισε (18), βοήσᾱσα (19), προσεχώρησεν (24, familiar from the caption), ἔστησε (25), ἐξηγήσαντο (27), and ἐδέξαντο (30). In initial readings of the passage it is enough for students to recognize the indicative forms as past tenses and the participles as denoting simple action. After studying Grammar 1, return to the reading passage and locate and discuss each form (Exercise 12a).

All of the first aorist forms in the passage can be explained from the rules given in Grammar 1 except ἔδοξεν, which is presented in Grammar 5; ἔστησε (25) is a regular first aorist formation, but students have not yet seen its present tense ἵστημι (stem στη-). The following forms are glossed and should not be discussed at this stage: ἐδύνατο (5, imperfect), προσδραμοῦσα (19–20, second aorist of προστρέχω), ἦρεν (20, liquid first aorist), and ἀνάβηθι (28, 29, irregular second aorist).

Translation

Lines 1–10

The next day as soon as day dawned, Dicaeopolis told them all to be getting themselves ready. And so the others got themselves ready at once, wanting to go as quickly as possible, and soon they were ready. But grandfather refused to go; for he was so old that he could not walk so far; and Melissa after walking so far the previous day was exhausted; and so the mother decided to leave her at home with grandfather. When the others were present, Dicaeopolis, leading (having led) them into the courtyard, approached the altar and, making (having made) a libation, prayed to Zeus to keep all safe (while) making so long a journey.

[παρασκευάζεσθαι (2): note the use of the present infinitive that describes a process ("to be getting themselves ready"). Note also the reflexive sense of the middle voice here and in παρεσκευάσαντο (3).

ἡ δε Μέλιττα . . . βαδίσᾱσα (5–6): note that the aorist participle always expresses simple aspect but that it here clearly denotes an action that took place prior to that of the main verb. It may therefore be translated "having walked."

Students should be able to deduce παρῆσαν "were present" (7) from ἦσαν glossed in line 4.

ὁ Δικαιόπολις ἡγησάμενος . . . ποιησάμενος. . . . (8–9): here too the actions expressed by the aorist participles clearly took place prior to the action of the main verbs, and the participles could be translated "having led" and "having made." It may be more natural, however, to translate with present participles in English; we give both versions here and in the paragraphs below.]

Lines 11–22

And so bidding goodbye (having bidden goodbye) to grandfather and Melissa, they set out, and soon, arriving (having arrived) at the gates of the city, they chose (took) the road to the harbor. The road was straight, leading (carrying) through the Long Walls; there were many people in (the road), and many wagons, and many mules also, carrying burdens either toward the city or from the city to the harbor. And Dicaeopolis hurries through the crowd wanting to arrive as quickly as possible. But Philip, although holding (he held) his father's hand, stumbled and fell to the ground. And his mother shouted (shouting, said), "Oh poor boy! What's happened to you?" And running (having run) toward (him), she lifted him up. But, being unhurt (having suffered nothing bad), he said, "Don't worry, mother; for although I fell, I'm all right." But his mother is still worried and examines the boy.

[To be deduced: κελεύσαντες (11), ἐνῆσαν (14), and βοήσᾱσα (19). In line 13, εἵλοντο is glossed to introduce the meaning "chose" in the middle voice. Give help as needed with the new meaning of φέρουσα "leading" in line 14. Students will remember ἅμαξαι (14) from the caption under the initial illustration.]

Lines 23–31

And while they are all waiting around not knowing (being at a loss) what they should do, a man approached driving a wagon. Seeing them waiting around in the road and in trouble (at a loss), he stopped the mule and said, "Tell me what the matter is, friends? Why are you waiting around like this? Has the boy suffered something bad?" And so they related everything, and he said, "Come here, boy, and get up on the wagon. And you too, lady, if your husband agrees (if it seems good to your husband) get up. For I too am going to the harbor." And they accepted his proposal, and going like this they soon arrived at the harbor.

[Encourage students to come up with their own translations of τὸν λόγον in the last sentence and remind them that they will need to find a translation for this word that fits the specific context in which it is used.]

Word Study

1. *mathematics:* μανθάνω (μαθ-) > μαθηματικός, -ή, -όν "fond of learning," "fit to be learned" > τὰ μαθηματικά "mathematics" (in our sense, since the Greeks considered that mathematics were the pattern of what is learnable).
2. *polymath:* πολυ- + μαθ- > πολυμαθής, -ές "learning or knowing much," "learned in many spheres."
3. *orthodoxy:* ὀρθός + δόξα (= "opinion") > ἡ ὀρθοδοξίᾱ "straight (= 'right') opinion."
4. *orthodontist:* ὀρθός + ὀδούς, ὀδόντος (= "tooth") = "one who puts teeth straight" (no such Greek word—an English coinage).
5. *orthopedics* or *orthopaedics:* ὀρθός + παῖς, παιδός = the branch of medicine concerned with "putting children straight" or curing deformities in children.

Grammar 1

Note that we do not give the emphatic translations, "I did loosen," "I did ransom," but teachers should remind students of these possibilities.

Exercise 12a

κελεύσαντες (11, participle, masc. nom. pl.); ὥρμησαν (12, indicative, 3rd pl.); ἔπταισε (18, indicative, 3rd sing.); βοήσᾱσα (19, participle, fem. nom. sing.); προσεχώρησεν (24, indicative, 3rd sing.); ἔστησε (25, indicative, 3rd sing.); ἐξηγήσαντο (27, indicative, 3rd pl.); and ἐδέξαντο (30, indicative, 3rd pl.). There is one other first aorist (ἦρεν, 20), but this is an asigmatic liquid form and will not be identified by students at this stage (see Grammar 4 later in this chapter).

Exercise 12b

Sets of forms of this sort are not provided in this handbook; teachers should check students' work carefully.

Exercise 12c

1. ἐδάκρῡσα 2. ἔβλεψα 3. ἐθαύμασα 4. ἤκουσα 5. ἐδεξάμην 6. ἐδίωξα 7. ἐνίκησα 8. ἐκήρῡξα 9. ἐκόμισα 10. ἡγησάμην 11. ἐβοήθησα 12. ἐδούλωσα 13. ἔπαυσα 14. ἐφύλαξα 15. ἔπεμψα

Grammar 2

Notes:

Exercise 12d

Sets of forms of this sort are not provided in this handbook; teachers should check students' work carefully.

Grammar 3

Notes:

Exercise 12e

ἦσαν (4), ἦν (5), ἦν (6), and παρῆσαν (7)

Exercise 12f

1. Dicaeopolis was not willing (refused) to lead his wife to the city.
2. The stranger, having entered, immediately asked for wine.
3. The priest, making a libation, prayed to the gods.
4. The women, although they had seen their husbands, did not stop shouting.
5. Go in, boy, and call your father.
6. Come here, boy, and tell me what you did.
7. After watching the dances, the girl hurried home.

8. The master told the slaves to be quiet, but they did not stop talking.
9. We were good, but you were bad.
10. The old man was so old that we all wondered at him.

Note the use of the present participle with its continuous aspect after ἐπαύσαντο in nos. 4 and 8.

Note the aorist infinitive expressing simple aspect in no. 8 (σῑγῆσαι might be translated "to shut up," expressing a simple action, rather than "to be quiet," which could in English imply a process or continuing state).

Note the translation of the participle in no. 7 with a temporal adverb, "*After watching*. . . . "

Exercise 12g

1. σπονδὴν ποιησάμενοι καὶ τοῖς θεοῖς εὐξάμενοι πρὸς τὸ ἄστυ ἐβαδίσαμεν.
2. ὁ πατὴρ τὸν παῖδα ἐκέλευσε οἴκαδε πέμψαι τὸν κύνα.
3. ἐγὼ μὲν σοὶ ἐβοήθησα, σὺ δὲ ἐμοὶ εἰς κίνδῡνον ἡγήσω. or ἐγὼ μὲν σὲ ὠφέλησα, σὺ δὲ ἐμὲ εἰς κίνδῡνον ἤγαγες.
4. τὴν μητέρα κάλεσον, ὦ παῖ, καὶ αἴτησον αὐτὴν δέξασθαι ἡμᾶς.
5. ὁ νεᾱνίᾱς νῑκήσας στέφανον ἐδέξατο.
6. ἐπεὶ εἰς τὸ ἄστυ ἀφῑκόμεθα (εἰς τὸ ἄστυ ἀφικόμενοι) πολλοὺς ἀνθρώπους ἐν ταῖς ὁδοῖς εἴδομεν.

Note that in no. 3 we use the emphatic, accented forms of the pronouns.

Here is material for an additional exercise if desired:

Change the following present forms into corresponding forms of the aorist:

κελεύομεν, πέμπουσι, ἀκούετε, λύεται, εὐχόμενοι, οἰκοῦμεν, προσχωροῦσι, δακρύουσα, δέχου, βαδίζομεν, βοηθεῖν, νῑκῶμεν, ἡγούμενος

Answers:

ἐκελεύσαμεν, ἔπεμψαν, ἠκούσατε, ἐλύσατο, εὐξάμενοι, ᾠκήσαμεν, προ-

σεχώρησαν, δακρύσᾱσα, ἐδέξω, ἐβαδίσαμεν, βοηθῆσαι, ἐνῑκήσαμεν, ἡγησάμενος

Trade and Travel

Illustration (page 144)

Detail of an Attic black figure cup, ca. 550 B.C. (London, British Museum).

For further reading, see *The World of Athens*, pp. 71–73, 180–185, and 230–231.

ΠΡΟΣ ΤΟΝ ΠΕΙΡΑΙΑ (β)

Caption under Illustration

"Dicaeopolis, having bade farewell to his wife, led Philip toward the ship": emphasize the second aorist participle and main verb.

Vocabulary

The entries for πλείων and πλεῖστος are not in alphabetical order; we wished to present the comparative before the superlative. Comparatives and superlatives are treated in Chapter 14, pp. 170–171; for the time being treat the forms simply as vocabulary items and do not go into a full explanation.

Verbs

The first paragraph and the first line of the second paragraph contain the following verbs in the imperfect: ἦν (1), ἔσπευδον (2), ἐκάλουν (3), ἐβόων (4), ἦγον (5), ἠπόρει (6), and ἔπῑνον(10). They are all glossed; students should be prepared to recognize the forms (present stem + augment + endings) from the Preview of New Verb Forms, but the forms need not be discussed fully at this stage. Wait until the next chapter, in which the imperfect will be formally treated, and use this reading primarily to consolidate students' ability to recognize first and second aorists.

Translation

Lines 1–9

In the harbor there was a very great crowd, and a very great uproar. For the people were hurrying in all directions; for the ships' captains were calling the sailors, telling them to carry the cargoes out of the ships, and the merchants were shouting loudly as they were receiving the cargoes and carrying them to the wagons; others having driven flocks out (of the ships) were leading them through the streets. And Dicaeopolis watching it all (everything) didn't know (was at a loss) what he should do and where he should look for a ship (that was) going to sail to Epidaurus. For he saw very many ships moored at the pier. Finally they all sat down in a wine-shop and asked for wine.

[ἀμάξᾱς (4): students are to recall this word from passage α.

Compound verb to be deduced: εἰσφέροντες (5).

Note that sometimes circumstantial participles can best be translated as independent clauses, as in the last sentence, where καθισάμενοι is translated "they sat down."]

Lines 10–18

And while they were drinking the wine, an old sailor approached and said, "Who are you, friends, and what do you want here (wanting what are you here)? For being countrymen (rustics) you seem to be at a loss. Tell me what is the matter." And Dicaeopolis, after relating everything, said, "Do you know if any ship here is about to sail to Epidaurus?" And he said, "Yes, certainly. My ship is about to sail there. And so follow me to the captain. But look!—here's the captain himself approaching at just the right time." And so speaking he led them to a young man at that moment (then) coming out of a ship.

Lines 19–26

And so Dicaeopolis approached and asked him if he was willing to take them to Epidaurus. "Yes, certainly," he said, "I am willing to take you there. But get on board quickly; for we are going to sail at once." And Dicaeopolis said, "For how much?" ("What's the fare?") And the captain replied, "For five drachmas." Dicaeopolis said, "But you are asking too much. I'm willing to give two drachmas." And he said, "No; I ask for four drachmas." Dicaeopolis replied, "Look—three drachmas; for I can't give more." And he said, "All right! Give me the money; and get on board quickly."

Lines 27–33

And so Dicaeopolis gave the money to the captain and bade farewell to his wife and brother. And Myrrhine, bursting into tears, said, "Guard the boy well, dear husband, and hasten to come home again as quickly as possible. And you, dearest boy, cheer up and with god's help return home soon with (having) your eyes healthy." So saying she turned away; and the brother led her back to Athens in tears.

[Note that the participle δακρῦσᾱσα (29) is an ingressive aorist, denoting the beginning of an action, "bursting into tears," while δακρυούσῃ (33) is present tense with continuous aspect.]

Word Building

1. guiltless
2. unworthy
3. unjust
4. unmanly, cowardly

Note that adjectives formed with α-privative (and other compound adjectives) have only two terminations, i.e., masculine and feminine forms are the same.

Further examples of formations with α-privative are:

ἡ τύχη "chance," "luck"; ἀτυχής, -ές = "unlucky," "luckless"; cf. εὐτυχής, -ές = "lucky"

φρήν, φρενός "mind"; σώφρων, σώφρονος (σῴ-ζω + φρην) =

"keeping one's mind," "sensible";
ἄφρων, ἄφρονος = "mindless,"
"foolish"; εὔφρων, εὔφρονος =
"well-minded," "kind."

Illustration (page 148)

Aerial photograph by the late Raymond V. Schoder, S.J.

Grammar 4

Notes:

Exercise 12h

1. ἔνειμα 2. ἤγειρα 3. ἤγγειλα 4. ὤτρῡνα
5. ἐσήμηνα 6. ἀπεκρῑνάμην

Grammar 5

Notes:

Grammar 6

Notes:

Exercise 12i

1. προσεχώρησα 2. ἐξέπεμψα 3. ἀπέφυγον 4. ἀπεκρῑνάμην 5. εἰσέπεμψα
6. ἀπέκτεινα 7. εἰσεκόμισα 8. συνῆλθον
9. συνέλαβον

Exercise 12j

1. The slaves lifted (having lifted) the
   stones (and) threw them out of the
   field.
2. The master drove (having driven)
   the oxen into the field (and) called
   the slaves.
3. The master sent the slaves away
   but stayed in the field himself.
4. Leaving (having left) the plow in
   the field, the slaves returned
   quickly.

5. The girl, seeing (having seen) her
   father, approached quickly and
   asked why he was not returning
   home.
6. But he answered that he must plow
   the field.
7. The young men did not run away
   but fought bravely.
8. The messenger announced that
   many (had) died in the battle.
9. The sailors prepared (having prepared) the ship (and) sailed out of
   the harbor.
10. The captain, fearing the storm, de-
    cided to return to harbor.

Ο ΚΩΛΑΙΟΣ ΤΑΡΤΕΣΣΟΝ ΕΥΡΙΣΚΕΙ

Title: "Colaeus Discovers Tartessus"

Verbs

This passage contains the following
verbs in the imperfect tense (glossed here
and to be treated in the next chapter):
ἔπλει (2) and ἐποιοῦντο (11).

Spelling

Note that in the passages adapted
from Herodotus at the ends of the chapters we retain his use of double σ where
Attic has double τ, e.g., κασσίτερον (10).
Students may use the forms with -σσ- in
the English to Greek translations that
follow, e.g., τέσσαρας in no. 3.

Translation

Lines 1–5
The first of the Greeks to reach
Tartessus were the Samians. (Of the
Greeks the Samians first reached
Tartessus). For a certain merchant
called Colaeus, setting out from Samos
was sailing toward Egypt, but a very
great storm arose, and for many days the
wind did not stop continually carrying
the ship toward the west. And finally,
having passed through (passing
through) the Pillars of Hercules (the

Straits of Gibraltar), they sailed out into the Ocean (i.e., the Atlantic) and so arrived at Tartessus.

[Tartessus was in the neighborhood of Cadiz.

διεκπερήσαντες (4): Ionic form as used by Herodotus.

Compound verb to be deduced: εἰσέπλευσαν (5).]

Lines 6–13

And the natives took them and brought them to the king, an old man called Argathonius. And he asked them who they were and where they had come from. And Colaeus answered, "We are Greeks; and while we were sailing toward Egypt, a storm drove us to your land." And the king, hearing all these things, was amazed, but he received them kindly and gave them very much silver and very much tin. And they stayed a long time in Tartessus and carried on trade. But finally, bidding goodbye to Argathonius, they sailed away and returned to Samos without any trouble (having suffered nothing bad).

[On Tartessus and Argathonius, see Herodotus 1.163–165. The trade opened up by Colaeus was developed by the people of Phocaea. Argathonius ruled for 80 years and died at the age of 120. His fabulous wealth came from the silver and tin. Silver came from the river Guadalquivir; tin, from Britanny and the west of Britain.]

Illustration (page 151)

Drawn from a vase found on Ischia (see page 143 of student's book), eighth century B.C. (Ischia Museum).

Exercise 12k

Encourage students to find as much vocabulary for the English to Greek sentences at the ends of the chapters as possible in the readings preceding them and not to rely on the vocabulary at the end of the book (e.g., in no. 6 students are to get the Greek for "carried on trade" from line 11 of the reading; the phrase is not included in the end vocabulary. Also some proper names will not be included in the end vocabulary.

1. ἐπεὶ ὁ Κωλαῖος οἴκαδε ἐπανῆλθεν, τοῖς Ἕλλησιν εἶπεν τί ἐγένετο.
2. πάντες ἐθαύμασαν, πολλοὶ δέ, ἀκούσαντες ὅτι ὁ Ἀργαθώνιος μάλα ὄλβιός ἐστιν, ἐβούλοντο εἰς Τάρτησσον πλεῖν.
3. ἔδοξεν αὐτοῖς εὐθὺς ὁρμῆσαι· καὶ τέσσαρας ναῦς παρασκευασάμενοι ἀπέπλευσαν.
4. πολλὰ καὶ δεινὰ παθόντες, τέλος εἰς Τάρτησσον ἀφίκοντο.
5. ὁ δὲ βασιλεὺς αὐτοὺς εὐμενῶς ἐδέξατο καὶ πολύ τε ἀργύριον αὐτοῖς παρέσχε καὶ πολὺν κασσίτερον.
6. οὕτως οὖν οἱ Ἕλληνες πολὺν τινα χρόνον ἐμπορίαν ἐποιοῦντο πρὸς τοὺς Ταρτήσσου πολίτας.

13
ΠΡΟΣ ΤΗΝ ΣΑΛΑΜΙΝΑ
(α)

Title: "To Salamis"

The noun is given in the vocabulary list.

The purposes of this chapter are:

1. Reading: (α) to begin the narration of the voyage of Philip and his father from the Piraeus to Epidaurus; (β) to record a nearly disastrous incident on board ship that leads to a narration by the old sailor who got them on board of the story of the Persian Wars, a narration that is prompted by their imminent arrival at Salamis; and in the reading based on Herodotus at the end of the chapter to record Xerxes' crossing of the Hellespont
2. Grammar: (α) to give a formal presentation of the imperfect tense; (β) to present the relative pronoun and relative clauses and to present third declension nouns and adjectives that show contractions between the stem and the ending when the σ at the end of the stem drops out between vowels
3. Background: to begin a study of the Persian Wars with an essay on the rise of Persia

Illustration

Based on an Attic black figure cup, ca. 550 B.C. (London, British Museum).

Caption under Illustration

"The ship was round, which was carrying grain and wine to the islands": the teacher will have to supply the meaning of στρογγύλη "round" (see note under second paragraph of the translation below); σῖτον will here refer to grain and not food in general (the sense in which the word has been used earlier); highlight the imperfect ἔφερε and use it to review the formation of this tense (see Preview of New Verb Forms and examples in Chapter 12β).

Vocabulary

The verb ἄγω was in the vocabulary for Chapter 2β and εἰσάγω was in the vocabulary for Chapter 11α; ἄγω is repeated here for its principal parts.

The verb ἐρέσσω is regularly spelled with double σ instead of double τ; its stem is ἐρετ-. We give the aorist in single rather than double σ.

For the forms of the reciprocal pronoun ἀλλήλων, see Reference Grammar, page 227.

For a paradigm of ταχύς, see Reference Grammar, page 221.

Verbs

Passage α contains the following verbs in the imperfect (glosses are kept to a minimum since students will be familiar with the formation of the imperfect from the Preview of New Verb Forms, from examples in Chapter 12β, and from the caption under the illustration at the head of this chapter): ἤρεσσον (5), ἔπλει (7), ἡσύχαζον (8), ἐσκόπει (8), ἦν (9), ἔφερε (10), ἐνῆν (10), ἐνῆσαν (11), ἐπανῆσαν (12), ἐπορεύοντο (13), ᾤκουν (13), ἐτέρποντο (13), ἦν (14), διελέγοντο (15), and ᾖδον (15).

Translation

Lines 1–6
Meanwhile the old sailor led Dicaeopolis and the boy on board the ship and told them to sit on the deck. Then the captain ordered the sailors to loose the cables, and the sailors having loosed the cables slowly rowed the ship toward the sea. Then after leaving land they spread the sails.

[For the word order in the phrase ὁ ναύτης ὁ γεραιός, see Chapter 5, Grammar 7a, p. 52.]

Lines 7–15

When the ship was sailing steadily and the sailors having stopped their work(s) were resting, Dicaeopolis examined all the ship. It was a round ship (the ship was round), not big nor fast but steady, which was carrying cargo to the islands. For there was grain in it and timber and flocks. And there were many people on board (in it), (being) countrymen, who, after selling their goods (cargoes) in Athens, were returning home; and others were journeying to relatives who lived in the islands. And all were enjoying the voyage (sailing)— for the wind was favorable and the sun bright—and they were either talking to each other or singing songs.

[στρογγύλη (9): "round," as opposed to a "long ship," ναῦς μακρά, or warship. Merchant ships were built with rounded hulls.]

Word Study

1. *nautical*: ναυτικός, -ή, -όν "of or belonging to sailors or ships."
2. *cosmonaut*: by simply pronouncing or transliterating ὁ κόσμος, students will see that it means "cosmos" or "universe" (the basic meaning of the Greek word was "order") + ὁ ναύτης = "person who navigates a spacecraft" (Russian term).
3. *aeronaut*: ὁ or ἡ ἀήρ, ἀέρος "air" + ναύτης = "navigator of a lighter-than-air craft."
4. *astronaut*: τὸ ἄστρον "star" + ὁ ναύτης = American term for no. 2 above.
5. *cosmology*: ὁ κόσμος + -λογίᾱ = "the theory of the universe" (coined, 1656).
6. *astrology*: ἡ ἀστρολογίᾱ = τὸ ἄστρον + -λογίᾱ = "study of the stars."

Grammar 1

Note the translations given for the imperfect: "I was loosening, I loosened." You could also give "I usually loosened." The important thing is to avoid confusion with the passive voice, "I was loosened."

Students should be given the imperfect of πλέω: ἔπλεον, ἔπλεις, ἔπλει, ἐπλέομεν, ἐπλεῖτε, ἔπλεον. Only forms in -εε are contracted in Attic (see the teacher's notes under Vocabulary for Chapter 6α on page 28 of this book for the present tense of πλέω in Attic).

Exercise 13a

ἔπλει (7), ἡσύχαζον (8), ἐσκόπει (8), ἦν (9), ἔφερε (10), ἐνῆν (10), ἐνῆσαν (11), ἐπορεύοντο (13), ᾤκουν (13), ἐτέρποντο (13), ἦν (14), διελέγοντο (15), and ᾖδον (15)

The verb ἐπανῇσαν (from ἐπανέρχομαι) in line 12 is also imperfect, but students have not studied this form yet.

Exercise 13b

Sets of forms of this sort are not provided in this handbook; teachers should check students' work carefully.

Grammar 2

Notes:

Exercise 13c

1. We were hurrying to the city, but you were resting in the house.
2. After leaving the harbor, the ship sailed (was sailing) toward the island.
3. When night fell, the wind became stronger.
4. Although we had fallen into danger, we were not afraid.
5. The Greeks used to honor the gods and love their city.
6. Waiting in the road, the women were talking to their husbands.
7. When the child was sick, the father took him to the doctor.

8. The farmers, having loosened the oxen, were leading (them) home.
9. When the sailors had rowed to sea, they raised the sails.
10. Shouting loudly, the merchants were carrying the grain out of the ship.

In no. 3, the coming of night is looked on as a simple event; the increase in the wind, as a process.

In no. 9, we translate ἤρεσαν "had rowed," because the aorist in a subordinate clause indicates time before the action of the main verb. This is a good time to point this out to students.

Exercise 13d

1. ἐλύομεν	ἐλύσαμεν
2. ἐλύοντο	ἐλύσαντο
3. ἐποίουν	ἐποίησαν
4. ἐφίλει	ἐφίλησε
5. ἐλάμβανε	ἔλαβε
6. ἠκούετε	ἠκούσατε
7. ἡγοῦ	ἡγήσω
8. ἐγιγνόμεθα	ἐγενόμεθα
9. ἐπέμπομεν	ἐπέμψαμεν
10. ηὔχοντο	ηὔξαντο
11. ἀφῑκνεῖτο	ἀφίκετο
12. ἐνῑκῶμεν	ἐνῑκήσαμεν
13. ἐβόᾱ	ἐβόησε
14. ἔπῑπτε	ἔπεσε
15. ἔλειπον	ἔλιπον

Exercise 13e

1. οἱ νεᾱνίαι τάχιστα ἔτρεχον πρὸς τὴν ἀγοράν.
2. ἐπεὶ οἴκαδε ἐπανῆλθεν ὁ παῖς, ἡ παρθένος πρὸς τῇ θύρᾳ ἔμενεν.
3. ἤδη ἔπλει διὰ τῶν στενῶν πρὸς τὸν λιμένα.
4. ἐγὼ μὲν οἴκοι ἔμενον, σὺ δὲ πρὸς τὸ ἄστυ ἐπορεύου.
5. ἐπεὶ εἰς τὴν νῆσον ἀφῑκόμεθα, οὐδεὶς ἡμῖν βοηθεῖν ἤθελεν.
6. τί ἐποίεις, ὦ παῖ, ἐπεὶ εἶδόν σε ἐν τῷ λιμένι;
7. ἆρ' ἐθεῶ τὴν ναῦν πρὸς τὴν θάλατταν ἐκπλέουσαν;
8. ὁ μὲν ναύκληρος μέγα ἐβόᾱ, ἡμεῖς δὲ αὐτὸν οὐκ ἐφοβούμεθα.

The Rise of Persia

Illustration (page 159)

Persepolis, Treasury, relief depicting an audience scene, with an Achaemenid king enthroned at center, attended by his Crown Prince standing behind the throne; Achaemenid Period, fifth century B.C.; excavated and photographed by the Persepolis Expedition of The Oriental Institute of the University of Chicago (Teheran, Archaeological Museum).

For further reading, see *The World of Athens*, pp. 10–17, and *The Oxford History of the Classical World*, pp. 38–49.

ΠΡΟΣ ΤΗΝ ΣΑΛΑΜΙΝΑ (β)

Illustration

Aerial photograph by the late Raymond V. Schoder, S.J., showing the site of the battle of Salamis seen from the island of Salamis facing east across to the mainland of Attica. The Greek navy formed up on both sides of the small island in the foreground and met the Persian fleet in the narrows, as it sailed in from the open sea (upper right in the photograph).

Caption under Illustration

"Look, the straits in which we fought against the barbarians": the new words, τὰ στενά, οἷς, and τοὺς βαρβάρους are in the vocabulary list. Attention to the relative pronoun will prepare students for the reading passage, which contains six further examples of relative pronouns.

Vocabulary

For the declension of τριήρης, see Grammar 4, page 164.

For the declension of ἀληθής, see Grammar 4, page 164.

Along with the adjective ἐκεῖνος we give examples of its placement outside the definite article-noun group, i.e., in the predicate position. See Chapter 5, Grammar 7b, page 52, and Chapter 14, Grammar 6, pages 178–179.

We include ψευδής and τὰ ψευδῆ in the vocabulary list for contrast with ἀληθής and τὰ ἀληθῆ.

Relative Pronouns

The nominative singular forms of the relative pronouns are given in the vocabulary list, and the relative pronoun is treated in Grammar 3 following this reading passage. Help students as necessary with the relative pronouns in the reading and after study of the grammar section come back to the reading and have students examine carefully the use of the relative pronouns (see Exercise 13f): αἵ, αἵ, ὅς, ὅν, οἷς, and ὅς.

Translation

Lines 1–8

And when they had sailed a short time, ten warships appeared, which were journeying to the Piraeus, returning from the islands. And so all watched the triremes, which were hurrying quickly through the waves. For the rowers, obeying the boatswain, struck the sea together. But when the triremes were out of sight (were no longer appearing), the wind became stronger (greater) and the sea became rough. And the people no longer enjoyed themselves, but the men were silent and women shrieked, praying Poseidon to bring them safe (to save them) to the harbor.

Lines 9–19

And a man who was sitting near Dicaeopolis got up and shouted (said shouting), "Poseidon, as it seems, is angry with us. For we are carrying an evil man in the ship, whom we must throw into the sea." And he was looking spitefully at those present. But the old man going up to him said, "Be quiet, man; for you are talking nonsense (saying nothing). For the wind is dying down (falling) now, and no longer is the

sea so rough. Sit down and keep still." And turning to Philip, he said "Don't be afraid (fear not at all), boy. For we're arriving at Salamis soon. For we're already sailing through the straits toward the harbor. Look, Dicaeopolis, (there are) the straits in which we waited for the fleet of the barbarians when we warded them off from Greece fighting for freedom."

[τῶν βαρβάρων (17–18): the Greeks regularly referred to the Persians and other non-Greeks as *barbarians*, which means properly those who do not speak Greek but say βαρ, βαρ.]

Lines 20–26

And Dicaeopolis said, "What are you saying, old man? Were *you* present at that battle?" And the old man said, "Certainly I was, being a young man and a rower in an Athenian trireme." And Philip said, "Are you telling the truth? Then you are very old, if you really took part in that battle. But tell us what happened." And he said, "It's a long story (the story is long), and, if you want to understand the events (the things that happened), I must relate everything from the beginning. And I, who was present, enjoy relating (the events). So listen."

[ἐκείνῃ τῇ μάχῃ παρῆσθα (20–21): note the use of the dative with the verb here.

The battle of Salamis took place in 480 B.C., fifty years before Philip's journey to Epidaurus—431 B.C.]

Word Building

These formations show how from one stem not only simple nouns and adjectives can be formed, but also compound nouns and verbs:

1. ἡ ναῦς: stem ναϝ, cf. Latin *navis*.
   ὁ ναύτης: sailor
   ναυτικός, -ή, -όν: naval
   τὸ ναυτικόν: fleet
2. ναυμαχέω: I fight at sea
   ἡ ναυμαχίᾱ: sea battle

ὁ ναύκληρος: ship's captain
ὁ ναύαρχος: admiral

The list could be considerably expanded, e.g.:

ναυαρχέω: I command a fleet
ἡ ναυαρχίᾱ: command of a fleet
ναυκληρέω: I own (am captain of) a
    ship

Grammar 3

Notes:

Exercise 13f

1. αἵ (1) refers to νῆες, fem. pl., and is
   the nominative subject of ἐπορεύοντο
   (2).
2. αἵ (3) refers to τριήρεις, fem. pl., and
   is the nominative subject of
   ἔσπευδον.
3. ὅς (9) refers to ἀνήρ τις, masc.
   sing., and is the nominative subject
   of ἐκαθίζετο.
4. ὅν (11) refers to ἄνθρωπον, masc.
   sing., and is the accusative object of
   ῥίπτειν.
5. οἷς (17) refers to τὰ στενά, neut. pl.,
   and is the dative object of the preposition ἐν.

Exercise 13g

1. The merchants who were sailing
   in that ship were not afraid of the
   waves.
2. The sailor to whom you gave the
   money led us into the ship.
3. The men whom you saw on the
   mountain were carrying grain to
   Athens.
4. Those slaves did everything that
   their master commanded.
5. The women to whom we were talking were not speaking the truth.
6. They honored all who fought for
   freedom.
7. That ship which you saw sailing
   away was carrying grain from the
   Black Sea.

8. The messenger whom you were
   listening to in the agora was not
   telling lies.
9. Were you not afraid of the barbarians whom Xerxes was leading
   against Greece?
10. Did you see that girl, at (with)
    whom the old man was so angry?

Grammar 4

The accusative plural masc./fem.
ἀληθεῖς is formed by analogy with the
nominative plural.

Exercise 13h

Sets of forms of this sort are not provided
in this handbook; teachers should check
students' work carefully.

Grammar 5

Notes:

Exercise 13i

1. We were marching for two days, but
   on the third day we arrived at the top
   of the mountain.
2. On the next day setting out for home
   we soon saw the walls of the city.
3. For a long time we were going down
   the mountain, but finally we sat
   down and rested by the walls.
4. The slave, going out at night, was
   looking for his master's dog. *or*
   The slave went out at night and
   looked for his master's dog.
5. The merchants, sailing away on the
   next day, arrived at the Piraeus
   within three days. *or*
   The merchants sailed away on the
   next day and arrived at the Piraeus
   within three days.

Exercise 13j

1. ἐκεῖνοι οἱ νεᾱνίαι πρὸς φίλους τινὰς
   ἐπορεύοντο οἳ ἐν τῇ πόλει οἰκοῦσιν.

2. οἱ νεᾱνίαι οὓς ἐν τοῖς ὄρεσιν εἴδετε
τὰ μῆλα πᾶσαν τὴν ἡμέρᾱν
ἐζήτουν.
3. ὁ ναύκληρος τὸ ἀργύριον ἐδέξατο ὃ
αὐτῷ παρέσχον.
4. διὰ τῶν στενῶν ἔπλει ἐν οἷς οἱ
Ἕλληνες τοὺς βαρβάρους
ἐνίκησαν.
5. ὁ ἱερεὺς ᾧ διελεγόμεθα τὰ ψευδῆ
ἔλεγεν.
6. ἡ ναῦς ἐν ᾗ ἔπλει τεττάρων ἡμερῶν
εἰς τὸν λιμένα ἀφίκετο.
7. τῶν γυναικῶν ἤκουον αἳ ἐν τῇ
οἰκίᾳ νυκτὸς ἐπόνουν.
8. τῇ ὑστεραίᾳ οἱ ναῦται πάντα
ἐποίησαν ἅπερ ἐκέλευσεν ὁ
ναύκληρος.
9. ἆρ' οὐκ ἐφόβου/ἐφοβεῖσθε ἐκεῖνον
τὸν γέροντα ὃς οὕτω μέγα ἐβόᾱ;
10. οἱ ξένοι, καίπερ σπεύδοντες, τῷ
γέροντι ἐβοήθουν, ὃς τοὺς βοῦς
ἐζήτει.

Ο ΞΕΡΞΗΣ ΤΟΝ ΕΛΛΗΣΠΟΝΤΟΝ ΔΙΑΒΑΙΝΕΙ

Title: "Xerxes Crosses the Hellespont"

Have students deduce the meaning
of the compound verb διαβαίνει.

Translation

Lines 1–5

Xerxes, wishing to subdue the
Greeks, prepared a very great army.
And when everything else was ready, he
ordered his generals to make a bridge at
the Hellespont, wanting to transport his
army into Europe. And so the generals
built a bridge, but a great storm arose
and destroyed and broke up everything.

Lines 6–10

When Xerxes learned what had
happened, extremely angry, he ordered
his slaves to whip the Hellespont, and he
told those who were whipping the sea to
say this: "O bitter water, our master
punishes you in this way; for you
wronged him though you had suffered no
evil at his hands. And King Xerxes will
cross you, whether you want it or not."

Lines 11–17

So he punished the sea, but those who
had built the bridge he put to death, cut-
ting off their heads. Then he told his
generals to build another bridge, very
strong. And when the bridge was ready,
Xerxes, coming to the Hellespont, first
wanted to see his whole army; and so he
climbed a hill from which he looked at
the whole infantry army and all the
ships. Then he ordered the generals to
transport the infantry into Europe. So he
led his host against Greece.

Exercise 13k

1. ἐπεὶ ὁ Φίλιππος πρὸς τὴν Σαλαμῖνα
ἔπλει, ὁ ναύτης ὁ γεραιὸς εἶπεν ὅτι
τῇ μάχῃ παρῆν.
2. ὁ Φίλιππος, ὃς μάλα ἐθαύμαζεν, "εἰ
τὰ ἀληθῆ λέγεις," ἔφη, "μάλα
γεραιὸς εἶ."
3. ὁ δὲ ναύτης ἀποκρῑνάμενος, "τότε
νεᾱνίᾱς ὤν," ἔφη, "ἐν τῷ ναυτικῷ
ἤρεσσον."
4. εἰ ἀκούειν βούλεσθε, ἐθέλω ὑμῖν
εἰπεῖν τὰ γενόμενα.
5. ἀλλὰ μακρός ἐστιν ὁ λόγος, ὅν με
δεῖ ἐξ ἀρχῆς εἰπεῖν.

14
Η ΕΝ ΤΑΙΣ
ΘΕΡΜΟΠΥΛΑΙΣ
ΜΑΧΗ (α)

Title: "The Battle at Thermopylae"

Students will recognize the proper name once they hear or read the title aloud.

The purposes of this chapter are:

1. Reading: to allow the old man on the ship to begin recounting the story of the Persian Wars, beginning with the battles at Thermopylae (α and β) and the Persians' advance by land to Athens and by sea to Phalerum; to provide at the end of the chapter a reading based closely on Herodotus' story of Ephialtes' treachery in leading the Persians up over the mountain and down the other side so that they could attack the Greeks from behind (see second paragraph of reading β)
2. Grammar: (α) to present the comparison of adjectives and adverbs and the constructions in which they are used; (β) to present the forms of the demonstrative adjectives οὗτος, ἐκεῖνος, and ὅδε, to show their use in the predicate position, and to show the correspondence of interrogative and indefinite adverbs
3. Background: to sketch the rise of Athens from the eighth century, to sketch the situation of Athens on the eve of the Persian Wars, and to describe Xerxes' invasion in 480 B.C.

Illustration

From a cup by the Painter of the Paris Gigantomachy, ca. 475 B.C. (private collection).

Caption under Illustration

"The Greeks, fighting most bravely, were warding off the barbarians": the superlative adverb (ἀνδρειότατα "most bravely") is a new form (to be treated in this chapter) and will need to be deduced or translated for students; both the superlative adverb and adjective will appear in passage α (18, 20). Make sure students recognize ἤμυνον as imperfect.

Vocabulary

Remind students that the stem of πράττω is πραγ- (see page 141).

The verb χράομαι has η where we would expect α, e.g., χρῆται and χρῆσθαι.

This and the following vocabulary lists in Book I contain many proper names. Teachers should not require students to learn all of these names, but we include them to help students connect the Greek words with the spellings of the names in English that students will be familiar with from other readings. In Book II we will list in the vocabularies only the names that we think students should learn and be able to use in Greek.

Comparative and Superlative Forms

Passage α contains the following comparative and superlative forms: μείζονα (4), πλέονας (5), μέγιστον (14), ἀνδρειότατα (18), ἀνδρειοτάτους (20), and ἄμεινον (22). Students have already had μέγιστος, πλείων/πλέων, and πλεῖστος in vocabularies 7α and 12β.

Translation

Lines 1–13

"When Xerxes, being (who was) king of the Persians, was preparing his expedition, intending to subdue all Greece, the leaders of the Greeks met at Corinth and considered what they should do. For a long time they were at a loss; for Xerxes had a larger army than all the Greeks and more ships. Finally they decided to ward off the barbarians at Thermopylae; for there by land the mountains lie so close to the sea that a few men can fight against many, and by sea there are narrow straits between Euboea and the mainland. And so the Greeks, learning that Xerxes was already marching against Greece, sent Leonidas, who was king of the Spartans, with (having) seven thousand hoplites. Arriving at Thermopylae, these prepared to ward off the barbarians from Greece.

[Encourage students to deduce the meaning of πρῶτοι ("leaders") in line 3 from their knowledge of the meaning "first."

εἶχεν (4): point out the irregular augment in the imperfect of ἔχω and encourage students to learn it; they will need to use it in exercises.]

Lines 14–25
"Xerxes, arriving at the narrows (of Thermopylae) with a vast army, remained inactive for four days; for he hoped that the Greeks would flee when they saw (having seen) the number of his host. But on the fifth day—for the Greeks still remained unmoved—he ordered his army to attack immediately. But the Greeks, fighting most bravely, warded off the barbarians. And finally Xerxes sent in the Persians whom he called the Immortals, who were (being) the bravest of his soldiers, expecting that these at least (γε) would easily conquer the Greeks. But when these too joined battle, they fared no better than the others, fighting in the narrows and not being able to use their numbers. And the King, watching the battle, leaped to his feet from his throne three times, as they say, fearing for his army."

[ἤλπιζε. . . . (15–16): students should have no trouble with the accusative and infinitive construction, which we gloss. It occurs also in line 21 below and in the tail reading, lines 11 and 13.

Students will recall ἀνδρειότατα (18) from its use in the caption under the illustration, and from this form they should deduce ἀνδρειοτάτους (20) in the

next sentence.

ἀθανάτους (20): the Immortals were a unit of 10,000 picked Persians, so called because when one was killed his place was immediately taken by a successor.]

Word Study

1. *Philip*: ὁ Φίλιππος = "lover of horses."
2. *George*: ὁ γεωργός = "farmer."
3. *Theodore*: ὁ θεός + τὸ δῶρον = "gift of God" (cf. late Greek θεοδώρητος, -ον).
4. *Sophie*: ἡ σοφίᾱ = "wisdom."
5. *Dorothea*: τὸ δῶρον + ἡ θεά = "gift of God."
6. *Ophelia*: ἡ ὠφελίᾱ (ὠφελέω = "I help," "I benefit").

As a continuation of this exercise on names, teachers might ask students to find and give the meaning of the following names of cities in the United States of America that are derived from Greek words:
1. Eugene (Oregon)
2. Emporia (Kansas)
3. Eureka (California)
4. Indianapolis (Indiana)
5. Philadelphia (Pennsylvania)

Grammar 1

The -έστερος, -έστατος formations on stems ending in -ον are by analogy with ἀληθέστερος, ἀληθέστατος.

Grammar 2

Notes:

Grammar 3

Notes:

Grammar 4

Notes:

Grammar 5

Notes:

Exercise 14a

1. μείζονα (4): comparative adjective modifying στρατόν (masc. acc. sing.), used with ἤ (5).
2. πλέονας (5): comparative adjective modifying ναῦς (fem. acc. pl.).
3. μέγιστον (14): superlative adjective modifying στρατόν (masc. acc. sing.).
4. ἀνδρειότατα (18): superlative adverb
5. ἀνδρειοτάτους (20): superlative adjective, used with the genitive τῶν στρατιωτῶν.
6. ἄμεινον (22): comparative adverb used with ἤ.

Exercise 14b

1. Very many of the Greeks fell fighting very bravely (very well).
2. The hoplites, although fighting very bravely, could not ward off the enemy, who were (being) more (in number).
3. The Greeks were braver than the barbarians and fought better.
4. The Greeks had far fewer (fewer by much) ships than the barbarians.
5. In that battle many of the Greeks died, but far more of the enemy.
6. The woman, being much more sensible than her husband, spoke more truly (more true things).
7. The Greeks, although being very few, prepared their weapons, intending to die as bravely as possible.
8. The barbarians, although they attacked very fiercely, could not conquer the Greeks.

In no. 4, remind students about the use of the dative to indicate possession.

In no. 8, remind students of the meaning "fierce" for ἄγριος (introduced

in vocabulary 5β); students will need to use this word in sentences 2 and 4 of Exercise 14c.

Exercise 14c

1. τοῖς μὲν Πέρσαις μείζων ἦν στρατὸς ἢ ἡμῖν (μείζονα στρατὸν εἶχον οἱ Πέρσαι ἢ ἡμεῖς), ἡμεῖς δὲ ἀνδρειότερον ἐμαχόμεθα.
2. οἱ ἄριστοι στρατιῶται τοῦ Ξέρξου ἀργιώτατα προσέβαλον ἀλλ' οὐδὲν ἄμεινον ἔπρᾱξαν ἢ οἱ ἄλλοι.
3. οἱ γέροντες οὐκ αἰεὶ σοφώτεροί (σωφρονέστεροί) εἰσιν ἢ οἱ νεᾱνίαι (τῶν νεᾱνιῶν).
4. οἱ ὁπλῖται τοῖς Πέρσαις καὶ ἀγριώτερον προσέβαλον.
5. ἔδοξεν ἡμῖν οἴκαδε ἐπανιέναι μᾶλλον ἢ ἐν τῷ ἄστει μένειν (μεῖναι).
6. ὁ ἄγγελος οὗ ἐν τῇ ἀγορᾷ ἠκούσαμεν ἀληθέστερον εἶπεν ἢ ὑμεῖς/σύ.

If necessary, remind students of μᾶλλον ἤ "rather than," in sentence 5 (see Grammar 3, page 172, and Grammar 4, p. 172).

In sentence 6 students may need to be reminded that ἀκούω is used with a genitive of the person heard.

The Rise of Athens

Illustration (page 175)

Attic black (and red) figure cup, ca. 510 B.C. (London, British Museum).

For further reading, see The World of Athens, pp. 5–15, and The Oxford History of the Classical World, pp. 31–35 and 38–49.

Η ΕΝ ΤΑΙΣ ΘΕΡΜΟΠΥΛΑΙΣ ΜΑΧΗ (β)

Illustration

Stone lion erected over the tomb of the members of the Theban Sacred Band who died at the battle of Chaeronea in 338

B.C., fighting against Philip of Macedon. The Lion of Thermopylae, which Herodotus saw, has disappeared, and so we have used the Lion of Chaeronea, which still stands in situ–an anachronism that we hope is justified by the fact that both lions were erected in memory of heroes fighting for the freedom of Greece.

Caption under Illustration

"The Greeks made a monument to Leonidas, since he had been a very brave man, a stone lion": words to be supplied or deduced: μνῆμα and λέοντα λίθινον. These words will not be glossed when they appear in lines 18–19 of the reading passage.

Vocabulary

We include αἱρέω (introduced in vocabulary 7α) in order to show its aorist.
We repeat πύλαι here (originally given in Vocabulary 6β), to add a new meaning, "pass" (through the mountains).
We include ὡς as an adverb meaning "how," which was introduced in vocabulary 6β, in order to allow a contrast to be made with ὡς as a conjunction meaning "as" or "when," introduced in this chapter.

Translation

Lines 1–10
"The next day the barbarians again attacked and fared no better than the day before. And so when Xerxes was at a loss, there came to him a man of the Greeks called Ephialtes, and he told him of the path that led (leading) through the mountains to Thermopylae. Learning this, Xerxes sent the Immortals by this route (this way), telling them to take the Greeks from behind. But the Greeks,

learning what was happening, at first were at a loss as to what they should do, but finally Leonidas decided to send the others away to Attica, but he himself remained at Thermopylae with (having) three hundred Spartiates, intending to guard the gates (i.e., the pass, which was thought of as the gates of Greece).

[Compound verb to be deduced: ἀποπέμψαι (8).]

Lines 11–22
"And so the barbarians attacked, and the Spartans fought against an enemy (enemies) who were many times their number and killed very many. And many of the Greeks fell including Leonidas himself (both many other . . . and . . .), after showing himself (becoming) a very brave (very good) man. And finally the Persians who had gone through the mountain arrived and attacked from behind. Then the Spartiates withdrew to the narrow (part) of the road and fought there until all fell. And after the war the Greeks buried the three hundred where they had fallen and made a monument to Leonidas, a stone lion, which it is possible to see even now. And they wrote this epigram on a stone tombstone:

O stranger, tell the Spartans that here We lie, obedient to their words.

[This chapter follows Herodotus' account of the battle closely and in places quotes his actual words; consequently the Greek is in places a little hard for students at this stage—see Herodotus 7.207–228.
αὐτὸς ὁ Λεωνίδης (13): see the discussion of the intensive use of αὐτός in Chapter 5, Grammar 5, pages 50–51.
Students will recall μνῆμα (18) and λέοντα λίθινον (19–19) from the caption under the illustration.]

Lines 23–32
"Meanwhile, by sea the Greeks waiting at Artemisium were guarding the straits, and fighting at sea they de-

feated the barbarians although they were more (in number) and warded them off. But when the barbarians had taken Thermopylae, the Greeks no longer guarded the straits but retired with their ships to Salamis. And by land they could no longer resist the barbarians but fled to the Peloponnesus, leaving both Boeotia and Attica to the enemy. And so the barbarians, advancing by land, were intending to attack Athens, and by sea sailing into Phalerum they lay at anchor in the harbor."

[ταῖς ναυσὶν ἀνεχώρουν (27): "with their ships," dative of military accompaniment, without a preposition; this usage should be pointed out to students, as it will recur in the readings.]

Word Building

1. There appears to be no difference in meaning between ὁ στράτος and ἡ στρατίᾱ (compare ὁ οἶκος and ἡ οἰκίᾱ).

   στρατεύω and στρατεύομαι: both words mean "I go on an expedition," "I campaign," "I wage war."

   τὸ στράτευμα: "expedition," "campaign," "army."

2. ὁ στρατηγός: "army leader," "general."

   στρατηγέω: "I am a general," "I command" (+ gen.).

   στρατηγικός, -ή, -όν: "of a general," "fit for command" (of persons).

   ὁ στρατιώτης: "soldier" (ἡ στρατίᾱ + -της agent suffix).

3. ὁ πόλεμος: "war."

   πολέμιος, -ᾱ, -ον: "hostile."

   πολεμικός, -ή, -όν: "of war," "fit for war," "warlike."

   πολεμέω: "I wage war."

Grammar 6

Notes:

Exercise 14d

1. αὗται 2. ἐκεῖνο 3. ταῦτα 4. τῶνδε 5. ταύτης 6. οὗτοι 7. ἐκείνου 8. ταύτῃ 9. οἵδε 10. τούτου

Exercise 14e

1. That tree is very big; I never saw a bigger tree.

2. Do you see these boys, who are chasing that dog?

3. Learning this (these things), the women at once called their husbands.

4. Why don't you want to use this plow? It is better than that (one).

5. αὕτη ἡ ὁδὸς κακῑ́ων ἐστὶν ἐκείνης· ἐκείνη δὲ μακροτέρᾱ ἐστίν.

6. ταῦτα ἰδών, ἐκεῖνος ὁ γέρων μάλιστα ὠργίζετο.

7. αὗται αἱ γυναῖκες σοφώτεραί (σωφρονέστεραί) εἰσιν ἢ ἐκεῖνοι οἱ νεᾱνίαι/ἐκείνων τῶν νεᾱνιῶν.

Students should be warned in no. 6 not to try to find a word for "things" but to use a neuter plural demonstrative adjective. This is something they should keep in mind for future readings and exercises.

Grammar 7

Notes:

Exercise 14f

1. Who are driving the oxen? Some old men are driving them.

2. Where is the king going? The king is going somewhere toward the mountains.

3. Where are the sailors? The sailors are somewhere in the harbor.

4. What are you suffering, children? Are you suffering some trouble?

5. What are you doing, father? Are you talking to this woman?

6. When do you intend to go to the city?
   I intend to go there sometime soon.
7. From where are you leading these
   flocks? I am leading them from
   that hill.
8. Where is my brother waiting?
   Your brother is waiting somewhere
   near the agora.

ΟΙ ΠΕΡΣΑΙ ΤΑ ΥΠΕΡ ΘΕΡΜΟΠΥΛΩΝ ΣΤΕΝΑ ΑΙΡΟΥΣΙΝ

Title: "The Persians Take the Pass
above Thermopylae"

Students will have to deduce the
meaning here of ὑπέρ with the genitive
("above"); previously they have been
given the meanings "on behalf of" and
"for."

Translation

Lines 1–7
   Xerxes, learning that there was a
path leading over the mountain, was
very delighted and sent Hydarnes, who
was (being) his best general, and the
men whom Hydarnes commanded.
They set out toward evening from the
camp, and Ephialtes led them. This path
begins from the river Asopus. And so the
Persians, after crossing the Asopus,
marched all night. Day was dawning,
and the Persians arrived at the top of the
mountain. At this point of the mountain
a thousand hoplites of the Greeks were on
guard.

Lines 8–15
   But these men did not see the Persians climbing up; for there were many
trees on the mountain. But hearing a
noise they learned that the Persians had
got up. And so the Greeks ran and were
putting on their armor, and immediately the Persians were there. But when

the Persians saw men putting on armor,
they were amazed; for although they
supposed that no one was guarding the
path, they met an army. And Hydarnes
marshaled the Persians for battle; but
the Greeks, supposing that the barbarians were intending to attack, fled to the
peak of the mountain and prepared to die
fighting. But the Persians took no notice
of the Greeks, and they went down the
mountain as quickly as possible.
[κατὰ τὸ ὄρος (8–9): have students deduce the meaning of κατά here ("on,"
not "down") from the phrase κατὰ τοῦτο
τοῦ ὄρους, glossed in line 6.
   It makes most sense to interpret the
participle ἐλπίζοντες (11) as concessive
("although").]

Exercise 14g

1. οἱ Πέρσαι ἐπεὶ τὰς Θερμοπύλας
   εἷλον, πρὸς τὴν Ἀττικὴν προ-
   σεχώρησαν.
2. οἱ δὲ Ἕλληνες ἀνεχώρησαν κατὰ
   γῆν τε καὶ θάλασσαν, τὴν Ἀττικὴν
   τοῖς πολεμίοις καταλιπόντες.
3. οἱ δὲ Ἀθηναῖοι, τάς τε γυναῖκας καὶ
   τοὺς παῖδας καὶ τοὺς γέροντας εἰς
   τήν τε Πελοπόννησον καὶ τὴν
   Σαλαμῖνα πέμψαντες, παρεσκευά-
   ζοντο κατὰ θάλασσαν μάχεσθαι
   (ναυμαχεῖν).
4. τοὺς οὖν ἄλλους Ἕλληνας ᾔτησαν
   εἰς τὴν Σαλαμῖνα ὡς τάχιστα πλεῖν
   καὶ βοηθεῖν.
5. οἱ δὲ Πελοποννήσιοι, οἳ τεῖχος
   ἐποίουν διὰ τοῦ Ἰσθμου, οὐκ
   ἤθελον τοῖς Ἀθηναίοις βοηθῆσαι,
   ἀλλ᾽ ὅμως τὰς ναῦς εἰς τὴν
   Σαλαμῖνα ἔπεμψαν.

In no. 1, the pluperfect "had taken"
is to be translated with an aorist, which
in a subordinate clause refers to an action that took place before the action of the
main verb (hence "had taken" in English).

15
Η ΕΝ ΤΗΙ ΣΑΛΑΜΙΝΙ
ΜΑΧΗ (α)

Title: "The Battle at Salamis"

The purposes of this chapter are:

1. Reading: (α and β) to allow the old man on the ship to continue his story of the Persian Wars with the narration of the Battle of Salamis, how it was arranged and how it was fought; to tell in the passage adapted from Herodotus at the end of the chapter how the Persians took the Acropolis at Athens after most of the Athenians had abandoned the city (this incident belongs chronologically between the first and second paragraphs of reading α)
2. Grammar: (α) to present the forms of three irregular second aorists (ἔβην, ἔγνων, and ἔστην); (β) to present the forms of contract verbs in -o- and of nouns of the second declension with similar contractions
3. Background: to present an essay on Aeschylus' *Persians* and a translation of Aeschylus' description of the battle of Salamis

Illustration

Drawing based on an Attic black figure cup by Nicosthenes, ca. 530–510 B.C. (Paris, Louvre). This painting clearly shows the helmsmen and bow officers; the ships are not triremes (which had 170 rowers); no complete Greek drawing of a trireme survives.

Caption under Illustration

"The Athenians, having embarked on their ships, were preparing to fight by sea": encourage students to deduce εἰσβάντες; they may recall the participle διαβάντες, which was glossed in line 5 of the reading at the end of Chapter 14.

Vocabulary

We give ὁ νοῦς here because its declension is given in Grammar 3 (the

word occurs in line 17 of passage α in the idiom ἐν νῷ ἔχω, which has been used since Chapter 4).

Θεμιστοκλῆς, -έους has dative Θεμιστοκλεῖ and accusative Θεμιστοκλέα.

Translation

Lines 1–7

"And so the Athenians were in the greatest difficulty, but Themistocles persuaded them not to yield to the barbarians but to fight for their freedom. And so they took the women and children and old men to the Peloponnesus and Salamis, leaving Attica and their city to the enemy. And they themselves, having boarded their ships, sailed to Salamis and prepared to fight by sea. [Compound verb to be deduced: προσέπλευσαν (6).]

Lines 8–13

"Meanwhile the generals of the Greeks met in Salamis and were so afraid that they wanted to flee away to the Peloponnesus; but Themistocles got up in the council and said that even now they could defeat the enemy; for fighting in the narrows the barbarians would not (will not) be able to use their numbers; and so they must force them to join battle there.

Lines 14–21

"He not only persuaded the other generals to fight by saying this, but he also sent a message secretly to Xerxes, saying that the Greeks were preparing to run away. And so Xerxes, when he learned that the Greeks intended to run away, wanting to destroy them as quickly as possible, decided to force them to fight at Salamis. And so he sent some of his ships around the island, telling his generals to guard the escape routes, and others he ordered to guard the straits so that the Greeks could no longer sail away."

Word Study

1. *monogamy*: ἡ μονογαμία (fourth century A.D.) = μόνος, -η, -ον +

γαμέω "I marry" = "the condition of being married to one person."

2. *monologue*: μόνος, -η, -ον + -λογίᾱ (coined 1668) = "a long speech made by one person."

3. *monochrome*: μονόχρωμος, -ον (Aristotle) = μόνος, -η, -ον + τὸ χρῶμα "color" = "a painting done in shades of one color."

4. *monosyllable*: μονοσύλλαβος, -ον (second century A.D.) = μόνος, -η, -ον + ἡ συλλαβή "syllable" (literally, "taken together") = "a word with one syllable."

5. *monograph*: μονόγραφος, -ον (third century B.C.) = μόνος, -η, -ον + ἡ γραφή (γράφω) = "a scholarly book on one specific subject."

Grammar 1

Notes:

Exercise 15a

εἰσβάντες (6, participle, masc. nom. pl.); ἀναστάς (10, participle, masc. nom. sing.); ἔγνω (16, indicative, 3rd sing.); διέγνω (18, indicative, 3rd sing.)

Exercise 15b

1. Don't you want to know what the messenger said?
2. The Athenians, learning that the barbarians had taken Thermopylae and were advancing toward Attica, were very afraid.
3. Themistocles, who was (being) a general, stood up and persuaded the Athenians not to yield to the enemy.
4. The Athenians, having sent the women and children to Salamis, went on board their ships.
5. Xerxes, learning that the Greeks intended to run away, wanted to force them to stand/stop and fight at Salamis.

6. Get out of the ship, boy, and stand on the pier.
7. The captain told the boy to stand up and get off the ship.
8. After going into the agora, the women stood and admired everything.
9. Apollo said at Delphi: "Know yourself."
10. Stop, friends, and wait for me!

On the walls of Apollo's temple at Delphi were inscribed the famous precepts: γνῶθι σεαυτόν "know yourself," i.e., know that you are a mortal, not a god; and μηδὲν ἄγᾱν "(do) nothing in excess," "be moderate in all things."

Exercise 15c

In these sentences students are to use the second aorists given in Grammar 1, with appropriate prefixes (εἰς-, ἀνα-, and ἐκ-).

1. εἰς τὴν οἰκίᾱν εἰσβᾶσαι, αἱ γυναῖκες ἐκαθίζοντο διαλεγόμεναι ἀλλήλαις.
2. σίγησον, ὦ παῖ· ἀνάστηθι καὶ βοήθησον (βοήθει) μοι.
3. εἰς τὸ ἱερὸν εἰσβὰς ὁ ἱερεὺς ἔστη καὶ τῷ θεῷ ηὔξατο.
4. ἐπὶ τὸ ὄρος ἀναβάντες ἔστημεν καὶ τὴν πόλιν (τὸ ἄστυ) ἐθεώμεθα.
5. ὁ γέρων τοὺς παῖδας ἐκέλευσε στῆναι καὶ ἀκοῦσαι/ἀκούειν.
6. μαθόντι τί ἐγένετο, ἔδοξέ μοι ἐκ τῆς οἰκίᾱς ἐκβῆναι καὶ τὸν πατέρα ζητεῖν.
7. αἱ γυναῖκες βούλονται γνῶναι διὰ τί δεῖ τὰς οἰκίᾱς καταλιπεῖν.
8. γνοῦσαι τί γίγνεται αἱ γυναῖκες εἰς τὰς ναῦς εἰσέβησαν.
9. οἱ στρατιῶται, οὓς ὁ Ξέρξης ἔπεμψε, ἐπὶ τὸ ὄρος τάχιστα ἀνέβησαν.
10. ἐπεὶ εἰς τὸ ἄκρον ἀφίκοντο, τοὺς Ἕλληνας εἶδον, οἳ οὐκ ἔστησαν ἀνδρείως ἀλλ᾽ ἀπέφυγον.

In no. 2, encourage students to use the prefix ἀνα- with the imperative στῆθι.

In no. 6, μαθόντι must agree with μοι ("it seemed good to me, having learned").

Aeschylus' Persae

For further reading, see *The World of Athens*, pp. 300–304, and *The Oxford History of the Classical World*, pp. 156–162.

Η ΕΝ ΤΗΙ ΣΑΛΑΜΙΝΙ ΜΑΧΗ (β)

Caption under Illustration

"The Battle at Salamis"

The topography of the battle and the movements of the fleets are controversial (Herodotus' account is obscure), but this plan (from Morrison and Coates, *The Athenian Trireme*, Cambridge, 1986), is clear and convincing.

Vocabulary

Notes:

Verbs

Highlight -o- contract verbs in this reading: ἐλευθεροῦτε (15), ἠλευθέρωσαν (42), and ἐδήλωσαν (43).

Translation

Lines 1–8

"And so all night the barbarians were rowing this way and that, guarding the straits and the escape routes, but the Greeks kept quiet, preparing to fight. But as soon as (when first) day dawned, the barbarians advanced (were advancing) into the straits, believing that they would defeat the Greeks easily, but suddenly they heard a very loud shout so that they were very afraid. For the Greeks, keeping (using) good order, were advancing into battle, and as they sailed (sailing) against the barbarians they shouted their battle song.

[Word glossed earlier in chapter: τοὺς ἔκπλους the escape routes.

Note that in προὐχώρουν (4) the vowel of the prefix and the augment have contracted and the breathing mark is retained. The form could also be written προεχώρουν.]

Lines 9–17

"And this is how (thus) the poet Aeschylus, who was present at the battle himself (also), describes the Greeks sailing against the barbarians:

The right wing led first in well-ordered discipline, and second the whole force came out against (them), and it was possible to hear a great united shout (much shouting together): 'O children of the Greeks, go on, free your fatherland, and free your children, your wives, and the shrines of your ancestral gods, and the tombs of your ancestors. Now all is at stake (now the contest is for all).'

[Note that ἡγεῖτο (12) is used without an object in the dative case and means "led," "advanced"; κόσμῳ (12) is a dative of manner and not the object of ἡγεῖτο.

θεῶν (16): usually disyllabic, but occasionally in poetry, as here, it undergoes synizesis and becomes monosyllabic.]

Lines 18–30

"So thus the Greeks began to attack the Persian force, and clashing in the straits they fought (by sea) few against many. And the barbarians, although they had very many ships, could not use all their ships together (at once). And the Greeks either damaged or sank the first of the barbarians' ships, attacking with such spirit that the barbarians turned, very afraid, and tried to flee away. Then there was tremendous confusion. For the barbarians' ships fell upon each other, some trying to escape from the battle, and others advancing into battle. And finally all the barbarians fled in disorder (using no order), and the Greeks pursued and sank very many ships; and everywhere there were wrecks, and everywhere corpses, so that it was no longer possible to see the sea. And so they fought until night fell.

[προσέβαλλον (18): the inchoative imperfect denotes the beginning of an action. Students should be alerted to this meaning of the imperfect.]

Lines 31–34

"Meanwhile Xerxes was sitting on a hill near the sea, watching the battle; for he believed that the Persians would win easily; for he was ignorant of the ways of (the things of) chance nor did he know what the gods had in mind, but he was always subject to (used) pride.

Lines 35–40

"But when he learned that the Greeks were winning and the barbarians fleeing away, he stood up and tore his robes. For he was in the greatest difficulty; for having lost his fleet he could no longer supply food for his land army, which was (being) very large. And so he ordered his generals to lead the land force to Asia by land, and he himself fled away, lamenting.

Lines 41–46

"And so the Greeks, having conquered the Persians, freed Greece. And what is more, in this action the Athenians provided the most ships and showed the greatest courage, so that it is possible to say truly that the Athenians saved Greece, and above all (not least) Themistocles, who as general (being general) of the Athenians was most responsible for the victory.

[This paragraph echoes the pro-Athenian bias of Herodotus' sources.

αἴτιος . . . τῆς νίκης (45–46): note use of the genitive with αἴτιος meaning "responsible for."]

Lines 47–52

"For the Athenians who died in this war, Simonides, the great poet (being the

best poet), wrote this epigram:
> If to die well is the greatest part of Virtue,
> Chance gave this to us above all.
> For striving to give freedom to Greece
> We lie here enjoying ageless glory."

Word Building

1. I gather, count, calculate, say; calculation, account, word
2. I turn; turning
3. I send; sending, escort, procession
4. I stay, wait; staying, delay
5. I hurry; haste, eagerness
6. I leave; left over, remaining

Grammar 2

Notes:

Exercise 15d

1. ἐλευθεροῦτε (15): 2nd person pl., present imperative.
2. ἐλευθεροῦτε (15): 2nd person pl., present imperative.
3. ἠλευθέρωσαν (42): 3rd person pl., aorist indicative active.
4. ἐδήλωσαν (43): 3rd person pl., aorist indicative active.

Additional Exercise (not in student's book)

Here are further sentences with -o- contract verbs:

1. ὁ στρατηγὸς τὰ ἀληθῆ γνοὺς πάντα τῷ δήμῳ δηλοῖ.
2. οἱ πολέμιοι τὴν πόλιν ἑλόντες τοὺς ἐνοίκους (inhabitants) δουλοῦσιν.
3. δεῖ ἀνδρείως μάχεσθαι, ὦ ἄνδρες, καὶ ἐλευθεροῦν τὴν πατρίδα.
4. τὴν ἀρετὴν δηλοῦτε ἣν αἰεὶ ἐδήλουν οἱ πρόγονοι.
5. οἱ ὁπλῖται, ταῦτα γνόντες, τοῖς πολεμίοις προσέβαλον καὶ πλείστην ἀρετὴν δηλοῦντες τὴν πόλιν ἠλευθέρωσαν.

Translations:

1. The general, learning the truth, shows everything to the people.

2. The enemy, having taken the city, enslave the inhabitants.
3. It is necessary to fight bravely, men, and set the city free.
4. Show the courage that your ancestors always showed.
5. The hoplites, learning these things, attacked the enemy, and showing the greatest courage they set the city free.

Grammar 3

Notes:

ΟΙ ΠΕΡΣΑΙ ΤΑΣ ΑΘΗΝΑΣ ΑΙΡΟΥΣΙΝ

Title: "The Persians Take Athens"

Lines 1–4
The Persians take the city deserted, and they find some of the Athenians (being) in the temple, stewards of the temple and poor men, who having barricaded the Acropolis, were warding off the attackers. And the Persians, taking up position (sitting down) on the hill opposite the Acropolis, which the Athenians call the Areopagus, besieged it.
[Note Herodotus' use of the historical present in the first sentence. Note also the predicate position of ἔρημον (1); "The Persians take the city (that is) deserted."
αἱροῦσι (1) and καλοῦσι (4): Herodotus does not use movable ν.]

Lines 5–11
And the Athenians, although suffering terribly (very bad things), refused to give in but defended themselves, so that for a long time Xerxes was at a loss, being unable to take them. But finally the

Persians took them like this; (for) some men got up where the place was sheer and the Athenians were not guarding (this point) but believed that no one could get up this way. And when they saw that they had gotten up onto the Acropolis this way, some threw themselves down the wall and died, and others fled to the temple. And the Persians first killed the suppliants, and then after plundering the temple set fire to the whole Acropolis.

[ἀναβεβηκότας (9): we have kept Herodotus' perfect participle, but the form need not be discussed at this stage.
τοὺς ἱκέτᾱς "the suppliants" (10): the Athenians would have taken sanctuary at the altar of Athena and thus, as suppliants of the goddess, were under her protection.]

Exercise 15f

1. ἐπεὶ ἔμαθον οἱ Ἀθηναῖοι ὅτι οἱ Πέρσαι πρὸς τὴν Ἀττικὴν προχωροῦσιν, ἀγγέλους πρὸς τοὺς Δελφοὺς ἔπεμψαν.
2. οὗτοι, εἰς τὸ ἱερὸν εἰσελθόντες, τὸν θεὸν ἤροντο τί δεῖ ποιεῖν τοὺς Ἀθηναίους.
3. ὁ θεὸς ἀποκρῑνόμενος εἶπεν· "ἡ Ἀθήνη οὐ δύναται ὑμᾶς σῴζειν. οἱ βάρβαροι αἱρήσουσι τὰς Ἀθήνᾱς. τὸ τεῖχος τὸ ξύλινον/τὸ ξύλινον τεῖχος μόνον ἀπόρθητον ἔσται."
4. οἱ ἄγγελοι τούτους τοὺς λόγους ἔγραψαν καὶ εἰς τὰς Ἀθήνᾱς ἐπανελθόντες τῷ δήμῳ ἤγγειλαν αὐτούς.
5. ὁ Θεμιστοκλῆς ἀναστάς, "ἀκούετε, ὦ Ἀθηναῖοι," ἔφη, "τί λέγει τὸ χρηστήριον· αἱ τῶν Ἀθηναίων νῆές εἰσι τὸ τεῖχος τὸ ξύλινον· αὗται γὰρ τὴν πόλιν σώσουσιν.
6. οὕτως εἰπὼν τοὺς Ἀθηναίους ἔπεισε μὴ εἴκειν τοῖς βαρβάροις ἀλλὰ κατὰ θάλασσαν μάχεσθαι.

16

ΜΕΤΑ ΤΗΝ ΕΝ ΤΗΙ ΣΑΛΑΜΙΝΙ ΜΑΧΗΝ

(α)

Title: "After the Battle at Salamis"

The purposes of this chapter are:

1. Reading: (α and β) to allow the old sailor to recount his involvement in Athenian naval engagements with the Persians around the Aegean subsequent to the battle of Salamis and his fighting in Egypt and Cyprus to the time of the peace with Persia in 449 B.C.; (β) to allow the old sailor to recount briefly his voyages as a sailor on merchant ships after his retirement from the navy and his resigned anticipation of death after a full life; and to give at the end of the chapter the alternative account of Xerxes' return to Asia after the battle of Salamis
2. Grammar: (α) to present the conjugation of verbs that add personal endings directly to the stem; (β) to present the declension of two third declension nouns, ἡ ναῦς and ὁ βοῦς
3. Background: to sketch the rise of the Athenian Empire from the time of the battle of Salamis to the outbreak of the Peloponnesian War

Caption under Illustration

"We saw the pyramids and the Sphinx and strange animals": students will be able to deduce πυράμιδας and Σφίγγα (-γγ- pronounced -ng-); ζῷα can be deduced from derivatives such as *zoology*; give the meaning of ἔκτοπα "out of place," "strange," "extraordinary." These words will not be glossed when they appear in the reading passage.

Vocabulary

Notes:

Translation

Lines 1–9

And so having finished his story, the sailor lay down on the deck, and Dicaeopolis and Philip were silent, wondering at all that he had said. And finally Philip said, "How bravely the Greeks fought! How brilliantly the Athenians led their allies! But you, what did you do after the war? Did you become a merchant and sail in merchant ships?" And he said, "No, for the war did not end, but we still had to fight against the barbarians for a long time. For the barbarians held all the islands and all Ionia."

Lines 10–11

And Philip said, "But how long (for how much time) did you have to fight? Were you involved in (present at) many battles?"

Lines 12–14

And the sailor stood up and went toward him and said, "Yes, certainly, my boy; I was involved in very many battles and sailed to many parts of the world with the allies. And we always defeated the barbarians."

Line 15

And Philip said, "But where (in the world) did you fight?"

Lines 16–26

And he (replied), "First at the beginning of spring (i.e., the spring following the battle of Salamis, 479 B.C.) we restored freedom to the Ionians; for we sailed with a hundred ships to Samos and having pursued the barbarians' fleet to Mycale, we disembarked onto the land and both defeated their army and destroyed their fleet. And when the Ionians knew that we were winning, they revolted from the Persians and helped us; and so they became free again. And the following year we sailed all over the Aegean Sea and drove out the barbarians; for we freed Cyprus and having sailed to the Black Sea we took Byzantium and many other cities; for nowhere could the barbarians stand up to us.

[Compound verb to be deduced: ἐξηλάσαμεν (23).]

Lines 27–31

"And later, when the Persians collected a very large army and two hundred ships and tried to force their way again into the Aegean Sea, Cimon, who was an excellent general, led us and caught them by the river Eurymedon and defeated them in a very great battle by both land and sea.

Lines 32–40

"And what's more we made a campaign to Egypt, and, helping the inhabitants, we drove out the Persians. For we sailed up the Nile, a very great river, which waters all Egypt in the summer and flows into the sea in seven channels; and we took Memphis, a very great city which lies on the Nile. And so for six years we remained in Egypt and saw many marvels; for the Egyptians do everything opposite to other men and use different customs. For among the Egyptians the women go to market, and the men stay at home and do the weaving.

Lines 41–50

"And we saw the pyramids, which are vast tombs of the kings of old and (we visited) the Sphinx, a very strange statue, half-woman and half-lioness. And what's more we saw unusual animals, crocodiles, which of all living creatures grow from the smallest to become the largest and most fearsome, and ostriches, huge birds, which cannot fly but run as fast as (no slower than) horses. But finally the Persians, having collected a vast force, attacked us and drove us out of Memphis. So for the first time we suffered a very great disaster; for we lost two hundred ships and scarcely escaped ourselves to Cyrene."

Word Study

Of these four words, no. 1 *dynamic*, no. 4 *dynasty*, and perhaps no. 2 *dynamo*

are directly derived from Greek words that are associated in meaning with the noun ἡ δύναμις (power, might, capacity), which is formed from the same stem as is the verb δύναμαι.

1. *dynamic:* from δυναμικός, -ή, -όν powerful, efficacious.
2. *dynamo:*—a coinage = a machine for creating electrical power; the suffix -*mo* is perhaps an abbreviation for motor, but it may be a more sophisticated coinage from the verb δυναμόω I put power into something, create power.
3. *dynamite:* = δυναμ- + termination -*ite*: so named by Alfred Nobel, the inventor of dynamite in 1867.
4. *dynasty:* derived from ὁ δυναστής a man with power, ruler; cf. English *dynast*, but *dynasty* has come to mean a line of hereditary rulers.

Grammar 1

Notes:

Exersise 16a

1. κατέκειτο (1): 3rd person sing., imperfect indicative of κατάκειμαι.
2. ἠπίσταντο (20): 3rd person pl., imperfect indicative of ἐπίσταμαι.
3. ἐδύναντο (26): 3rd person pl., imperfect indicative of δύναμαι.
4. δύνανται (46): 3rd person pl., present indicative of δύναμαι.

Exercise 16b

1. Stranger, tell the Spartans that here We lie obedient to their words.
2. Do you know why the allies cannot come to our aid?
3. The woman did not know that her husband had died in that battle.
4. This island lay so close to the mainland that we crossed to there easily.
5. In no sea battle could the barbarians beat the Greeks.

6. The majority of the women are helping their husbands, but two lie in the house talking to each other.
7. Although fighting very bravely, the Spartans were not able to ward off the barbarians.
8. Why aren't you working, young man, but lying so lazily?
9. Knowing that the master was approaching, the slaves who were lying in the field stood up and began to work.
10. Know this, that you are not able to deceive the gods.

The epitaph on the Spartan dead at Thermopylae in no. 1 is attributed to Simonides. The three hundred who died fighting with Leonidas were buried at Thermopylae—see Chapter 14; the "stranger" is the passer-by who pauses to read the epitaph. In Greek epitaphs the dead often speak from their tombs and address those who read their words.

In no. 4, ἐπέκειτο from ἐπίκειμαι is to be deduced; cf. πρόσκειται (14α:7).

In no. 6, note αἱ πολλαί = "the majority"; so οἱ πολλοί and τὰ πολλά = "most (of)."

In no. 9, note the irregular augment on εἰργάζοντο and the inchoative meaning of the verb here ("began to work").

Exercise 16c

1. οὐ δυνάμεθα σοι (ὑμῖν) βοηθεῖν· ὁ γὰρ πατὴρ ἡμᾶς ἐκέλευσε πρὸς τὸν ἀγρὸν ἰέναι.
2. οὐκ ἐπισταμένη διὰ τί οὐκ ἐπανῆλθεν ὁ ἀνήρ, ἡ γυνὴ μάλιστα ἐφοβεῖτο.
3. οἱ ναῦται οἳ ὑπὸ ἐκείνῳ τῷ δένδρῳ ἔκειντο ἀνέστησαν καὶ (ἀναστάντες) πρὸς τὸν λιμένα ἔσπευδον.
4. οὐ δυνάμενοι τὰ μῆλα εὑρεῖν, οἱ νεανίαι ἐπὶ τὸ ὄρος ἀνέβησαν καὶ (ἀναβάντες) πᾶσαν τὴν ἡμέρᾱν ἐζήτουν.
5. οὐδεὶς ἐπίσταται διὰ τί ἡ γυνὴ τὸν οἶκον λιποῦσα πρὸς τὸ ἄστυ ἦλθεν.

The Athenian Empire

Illustration (page 201)

The Athenian tribute lists are among the most valuable epigraphical records of ancient Athens. Running from 454 to 415 B.C., when the system of tribute was abolished, they enable us to reconstruct the extent and organization of the Empire and the relative importance of its members. The lists were engraved on a huge block of Pentelic marble erected on the Acropolis, and over a hundred fragments survive. The lists were reconstructed and interpreted by Professors West and Meritt in 1927–1928. The amounts payed are in drachmas, written in Attic alphabetic numerals. (Athens, National Archaeological Museum)

For further reading, see *The World of Athens*, pp. 18–26 and 232–241, and *The Oxford History of the Classical World*, pp. 124–136.

META THN EN THI ΣΑΛΑΜΙΝΙ ΜΑΧΗΝ (β)

Caption under Illustration

"I saw Mount Etna throwing rivers of fire toward the heavens": encourage students to deduce τὸ Αἰτναῖον ὄρος.

Both Pindar (*Pythian* 1.21–28) and Aeschylus (*Prometheus Bound* 366–369) describe the major eruption of Mount Etna that took place probably in 475/4 B.C. Pindar describes it as follows:

From its depths belch forth holy springs of unapproachable fire; and in the daytime its rivers pour out a fiery stream of smoke; but in the darkness red flames roll rocks and carry them with a crash into the deep flats of the sea.

Vocabulary

Notes:

Translation

Lines 1–2

But Philip (asked), "After suffering such a disaster didn't you cease from the war?"

Lines 3–10

And the sailor said, "Certainly not (least of all); for nothing could reduce the spirit of the Athenians. And so soon Cimon led the fleet to Cyprus and again defeated the Persians, but he himself was killed (died) besieging a certain city. And so we sailed away for home, grieving. And the following year the people made peace with the king (of Persia). So great were the deeds we accomplished fighting against the barbarians. And so a very great trial lies before you, my boy; for you must become worthy of your ancestors (fathers)."

[After he returned from ostracism, Cimon was sent with 200 ships to help the Greeks in Cyprus, where the Persians were attempting to re-establish control; he died during the siege of Cition; before sailing home the Greek fleet succeeded in raising the siege of Cition and defeated the Phoenician fleet at Salamis. The Athenians made peace with the Persian king—the Peace of Callias—the following year (449 B.C.) on very favorable terms.

τῷ βασιλεῖ (8): note this use of the dative of association without a preposition; πρός + acc. could also be used.

εἰργασάμεθα (8): students have met this verb (ἐργάζομαι) with the meaning "I work"; we gloss it here because of the irregular augment and because of the different meaning in this context— "accomplish."]

Lines 11–13

And Philip said, "You are speaking the truth, old man; and if god will be propitious, I will try to become a good man, worthy of my ancestors (fathers). But what did you do in peacetime?"

Lines 14–21

And the old man said, "I was no longer young (a young man) and I did not enjoy such strength that I could row in the fleet. And so, serving in merchant ships, I sailed to many parts of the world. For I (both) went to Sicily, where I saw Mount Etna throwing rivers of fire toward the heavens, and I sailed to Scythia, where in winter the frosts are so severe that even the sea freezes. And now being very old I make some little voyages around the islands and wait for death contentedly."

[Word glossed earlier in chapter: ὁλκάσι merchant ships.]

Lines 22–24

And Philip said, "You have seen much in your long life and suffered much too. For Odysseus himself wandered no further than you."

Lines 25–27

But the old man looking toward the land got up and said, "Look, we are already reaching (present at) the harbor. And so farewell. For I must hurry and help the other sailors."

Lines 28–29

So speaking, he went off to the bow (of the ship), and they stayed pondering all that he had said.

[Compound verb to be deduced: ἀπέβη.]

Lines 30–32

And when they arrived inside the deep harbor,
They took down the sails, and put them in the black ship
Nimbly, and the ship they rowed forward with the oars into the anchorage.

[Quoted from Homer Iliad 1.432–433, 435; note that Homer does not augment the aorist ἵκοντο; note the absence of augment and the double σ in the aorist προέρεσσαν.]

Lines 33–35

And so when the ship was moored at the pier, the people disembarked onto the land. And after disembarking, some hurried home, and others walked into the city looking for a tavern.

Word Building

1. spiritless, despondent; I am despondent; lack of spirit
2. cheerful; I am cheerful; cheerfulness
3. eager; I am eager; eagerness

Grammar 2

Notes:

Exercise 16d

1. αἱ μακραὶ νῆες
2. οἱ ἀληθεῖς λόγοι
3. τοῦ σώφρονος ποιητοῦ
4. τῷ μεγάλῳ βοΐ
5. τῆς καλλίονος πόλεως
6. τοῦτον τὸν νεανίαν
7. ταύτης τῆς νεώς
8. αὗται αἱ γυναῖκες
9. τοῖς σώφροσιν ἱερεῦσιν
10. τῇ μείζονι νηΐ
11. τοῦ μεγάλου βασιλέως
12. τοῖς ψευδέσι μύθοις
13. οἱ μεγάλοι βόες
14. τοῖσδε τοῖς τείχεσιν

Ο ΞΕΡΞΗΣ ΠΡΟΣ ΤΗΝ ΑΣΙΑΝ ΑΝΑΧΩΡΕΙ

Title: "Xerxes Withdraws to Asia"

Translation

Lines 1–8

There is also this other story, that when Xerxes, marching away from Athens reached Eion, he no longer journeyed by land but entrusted (entrusts) the army to Hydarnes to lead to the Hellespont, and he himself embarked on a ship and sailed to Asia. But on the voyage (for him sailing) the wind became stronger, and the sea became rough. And the ship, carrying very many men of the Persians, who were accompanying Xerxes, was in danger. And the king, being very frightened, asked the helmsman if there was any (means of) safety for them. And he said, "Master, there is no hope of safety, unless we get rid of some of the many passengers."

[ἐπιτρέπει (2): note the use of the historical present in the same sentence with an aorist (ἐπεὶ . . . ἀφίκετο, 1) and imperfect (ἔπλει, 3); these are the tenses used by Herodotus, who quite freely mixes his tenses in this way. In English, past tenses would be used throughout.

πλέοντι . . . αὐτῷ (4): dative of the person concerned.]

Lines 9–14

And when Xerxes heard this, he said, "Persians, now you must show whether you love your king; for on you, it seems, depends (is) my salvation." So he spoke, and they bowed down to him and threw themselves into the sea, and the ship thus lightened brought the king safely to Asia. And when he disembarked onto the land, Xerxes acted as follows (did this); because he had saved the king, he gave the helmsman a golden crown, but because he had destroyed many of the Persians, he cut off his head.

Illustration (page 207)

A temple was planned for this bastion on the southwest side of the Acropolis looking down toward Salamis in 449 B.C., the year Athens made peace with Persia, to commemorate Greek victories in the Persian Wars, but the temple was not built until 427–424. Callicrates was the architect.

Exercise 16e

1. μετὰ τὴν μάχην ὅ τε Ξέρξης καὶ οἱ στρατηγοὶ ὀλίγας τινὰς ἡμέρας ἐν τῇ Ἀττικῇ μείναντες πρὸς τὴν Βοιωτίαν ὥρμησαν.
2. ὁ βασιλεὺς τὸν Μαρδόνιον ἐκέλευσε τὸν μὲν χειμῶνα ἐν τῇ Θετταλίᾳ

μένειν, ἅμα δὲ ἦρι ἀρχομένῳ ἐπὶ
τὴν Πελοπόννησον προχωρεῖν.
3.   ἐπεὶ εἰς τὴν Θεσσαλίᾱν ἀφίκοντο, ὁ
μὲν Μαρδόνιος τοὺς ἀρίστους τῶν
στρατιωτῶν ἐξελέγετο, ὁ δὲ Ξέρξης
αὐτοὺς ἐκεῖ καταλιπὼν πρὸς τὸν
Ἑλλήσποντον ὡς τάχιστα
ἐπορεύετο.
4.   τῷ ἄλλῳ λόγῳ ὃν λέγουσι περὶ τοῦ
νόστου τοῦ Ξέρξου οὐ δυνάμεθα
πιστεύειν.
5.   οἱ τὰ ἀληθῆ ἐπιστάμενοι (ἐκεῖνοι οἳ
τὰ ἀληθῆ ἐπίστανται) λέγουσιν ὅτι

πρὸς τὴν ᾿Ασίᾱν κατὰ γῆν
ἀναχωρῶν εἰς τὸν Ἑλλήσποντον
πέντε καὶ τεσσαράκοντα ἡμερῶν
ἀφίκετο.

For no. 2, students may need to be
reminded that χειμών can mean
"winter" as well as "storm" (see Vocabulary 7β and passage 16β:18). In 16β the
word is used in the genitive to express
time when; here it must be in the accusative to express duration of time.

REFERENCE GRAMMAR

This section of the student's book presents some material on syllables, accents, enclitics, and proclitics that is not included in the grammar sections of the book itself and that students will need to become familiar with in order to understand and handle accents. Otherwise, the Reference Grammar presents a systematic arrangement of the paradigms of forms and the grammatical information that are included in the chapters themselves. Often additional linguistic information is supplied. The general order of the material is as follows: definite article (2), nouns (3–6), adjectives and participles (7–15), pronouns (16–22), adverbs (23–25), numbers (26), prepositions (27), verbs (28–35), uses of the article (36), uses of the cases (37), agreement (38), word order (39), and uses of participles (40).

Teachers should periodically guide students through the material in the Reference Grammar to acquaint them with what is there and how it is arranged and to point out the different kinds of information contained in this section of the book.

Syllables and Accents (page 208)

Teachers should be aware of the fact that what we say here applies to accentuation and not necessarily to scansion of poetry (a matter that is not dealt with in this book).

Nouns of the First Declension (pages 211–212)

Note that we now give ὁ νεᾱνίᾱς as an example instead of ὁ Ξανθίᾱς, in order to show the plural.

Participles (pages 221–223)

Note that in the paradigm of the first aorist participle we divide between the extended participial stem λῡσαντ- and the endings. This is effective pedagogically in that it clearly shows the third declension endings. In the second aorist participle, however, we divide after the root λαβ-. This is also effective pedagogically in that it clearly shows the similarity between the forms of the second aorist participle and those of the present participle, e.g., the present participles of εἰμί and λῡω shown on pages 221–222.

Illustration (page 243)

After an Attic red figure cup, ca. 480 B.C. (Basel, Antikenmuseen).

VOCABULARIES

GREEK TO ENGLISH VOCABULARY

This vocabulary list contains all of the words that are in the vocabulary lists in the chapters and the words presented in grammar sections that need to be learned (e.g., the irregular comparatives and superlatives and the numbers). It also contains all of the compound verbs that occur in the readings and of which students are expected to deduce the meaning. Students should always be encouraged to deduce the meaning of these verbs when they meet them in the readings and not have recourse to the Greek to English Vocabulary, but we have included the words in the vocabulary for purposes of reference. The Greek to English Vocabulary also contains all words that are glossed once in a chapter and used again later in that chapter (in the exercises or readings) but not glossed again. For the most part students will remember these words from their initial encounter with them in the reading where they are glossed, but we include them in the Greek to English Vocabulary for reference.

We do not include in the Greek to English Vocabulary words that are glossed once in a chapter and do not occur again in that chapter or in a vocabulary list in a subsequent chapter.

The numbers following definitions of words refer to the chapters in which the words are included in vocabulary lists or grammar sections.

Note that to facilitate alphabetization we list words in a slightly different way from that used in the vocabulary lists in the chapters. For nouns we give the nominative, genitive, and definite article. For adjectives we spell out the nominative masculine, feminine, and neuter. For verbs we give the present and the aorist indicatives (omitting the participles), and occasionally the imperfect (where the aorist is lacking or not generally used).

We give the second aorist infinitives of verbs in which the aorist stem is from a different root from that of the present, e.g., ἰδεῖν, and we then identify the corresponding verb in the present tense, in this case, ὁράω.

ENGLISH TO GREEK VOCABULARY

The English to Greek Vocabulary is not limited to words needed in the English to Greek translation exercises; it instead contains a complete reverse listing of all of the words in the Greek to English Vocabulary. This complete list will make it easier for teachers to make up additional exercises, and it will enable students to write Greek using almost any of the words that they have met in the readings.

The English to Greek Vocabulary is intended only as a reminder of the Greek word. For full information about any given Greek word, students will have to look the word up in the Greek to English Vocabulary. Students should also be urged always to look back at the readings and the grammar sections to refresh their minds on how a given word is used. Students will also have to learn to discriminate between words in entries where more than one Greek word is given, e.g., between ἐμπίπτω and προσβάλλω under "attack" and between βαδίζω, βαίνω, ἔρχομαι, and πορεύομαι under "go." Students should always be encouraged to consult the readings in making these discriminations.

SUBJECT INDEX

WORD STUDY INDEX

The page references are to the Word Study sections in the student's book.

WORD BUILDING INDEX

The page references are to the Word Building sections in the student's book.